The
New
Society

The New Society

Anthony Westell

McClelland and Stewart

ISBN: 0-7710-8945-7

The Canadian Publishers
McClelland and Stewart Limited
25 Hollinger Road
Toronto, Ontario M4B 3G2

Excerpts from "Conversations with the
Prime Minister," produced by CTV News,
copyright CTV Television Network Ltd.,
1975, reproduced with the permission of
the copyright holder.

Canadian Cataloguing in Publication Data
Westell, Anthony, 1926-
   The new society

Bibliography: p.
Includes index.
ISBN 0-7710-8945-7 bd.

1. Canada—Politics and government—1963-   *
2. Canada—Economic conditions—1965-   *
3. Canada—Economic policy.   4. Internationalism.
I. Title.

FC625.W48   971.06'44   C77-001190-X
F1034.2.W48

Printed and bound in Canada

Contents

To Dan and Tracy,
journalism students

Introduction

The title for this book is taken from a statement made by Prime Minister Pieire Trudeau during a television broadcast in December 1975: "I will be speaking to you again in the coming months about the new kind of society we will need to create in response to the new economic circumstances in which we are living, here in Canada and throughout the world." When he sought subsequently to elaborate on that commonplace idea, he was silenced by a storm of protest. The critics seemed to imagine that he was planning to drive the nation by forced marches to some bleak socialist society, or worse. But all he was really saying was that new problems call for new solutions which will change the society in which we live. Of course they will, and it is in that sense that the phrase "new society" is used in this book. It refers to a process of continuing change rather than to an ultimate goal.

Twenty years ago, in the middle fifties, we could hardly have imagined the way in which we live today. As a society, we are far richer and more permissive. Our attitudes and priorities have changed. We have a different view of the world. All this is reflected in our politics, which are new in style and content. While the upheavals of the sixties have subsided, they have left among the young a residue of ideas and expectations that ensure, not revolution as was once predicted, but continuing change. The new generation will have to grapple with the implications of the enlarging role of the state in the economy and with the emergence of what has been called the post-industrial society.

In addition, while we cannot foresee, far less control, events in the world around us, it seems certain that shifts in the balance of economic and military power will force Canadians to change their national expectations and priorities. So the question is not whether there will be a new society, but what sort of society it will be. I seek to engage the question in this book by identifying in the confusing rush of events some of the underlying political, economic, social, and cultural problems, and by suggesting, if not specific solutions, at least the direction in which we ought to look for solutions.

9

Only a journalist would be so foolhardy as to invade so many areas of specialized knowledge. As John Porter remarked severely in *The Vertical Mosaic*, reporters are prepared to write about almost anything, although we have no specialized academic training. "Perhaps no other occupational group in modern society appropriates to itself a role which requires all-seeing wisdom in so many spheres," he says. The put-down is well taken, but if Canadians are to understand current problems and make informed decisions about the future, somebody has to try to bring together the many separate strands of expert knowledge and opinion and weave a pattern. If not brash journalists, who will? As Trudeau discovered, it is dangerous for politicians to speculate about the future, and academics usually prefer to remain within the limits of their own disciplines. A journalist has no reputation for learning or wisdom to lose, and if I provoke experts to dispute my facts and opinions, the main purpose of this book, which is to encourage debate, will have been served.

As a journalist, I gather and interpret information published by others rather than undertaking original research to produce new knowledge. The reader will find I have quoted many books and reports. A partial bibliography is provided, but I must make clear that I have selected the quotations that support my interpretation, and I am solely responsible for the opinions that emerge in the book.

Similarly, I have had the advantage of discussing ideas with colleagues and students at Carleton University, where I teach public affairs journalism and have been a Visiting Fellow in the Institute of Canadian Studies, but my conclusions are my own.

The editors of the Toronto *Star* have encouraged me to explore in my column on the editorial page some of the ideas discussed in this book. That column is properly labelled as my "Opinion," which is not necessarily that of the *Star*.

Journalists are not objective. We are conditioned by upbringing, education, and experience, and the best we can do is to strive to be fair. But I should point out the perspective from which I approach this book. From about the age of twenty, I have thought of myself as a socialist, although I have tried not to let that influence my reporting of politics and government. I hope that this declaration will not prejudice the reader because for me socialism is an end, not a means. I seek equality and fraternity in liberty by a process of evolution rather than revolution, by improving the existing social and economic order rather than by demolishing capitalism to build a new Jerusalem on the rubble. Some of the means to the end are suggested in this book, and the reader may conclude I am better described as a social democrat than as a socialist – but so, I think, are the great majority of modern "socialists" who have had to revise their ideas about the virtues of public ownership, the evils of private profit, and the perfectability of man. It will take a little longer than once we thought.

So I hope the reader will accept that I approach the new society with a point of view that is clear but not doctrinaire – and I fully expect that my interpretations and opinions will enrage as many social democrats as those who regard themselves as liberals or conservatives.

Above all, I approach the new society as a democrat. I am concerned first and foremost with the institutions through which we discuss social goals and seek to find a consensus on which to base public policy. I have my own ideas on what policies we should follow and I hope to persuade others to share my views, but I believe it far more important to try to ensure that our institutions enable the collective judgement to prevail. If our democratic institutions fail, no goals of mine for a new society will be of much importance.

PART ONE:
THE NEW POLITICS

1

The State

COLLECTIVISM

I expect the new society to develop along trends already well established in all industrial democracies. These trends run strongly toward collectivism – that is, toward a society in which the state plays the central role in planning the economy and setting social priorities. We are already well down that road. Governments are increasingly asserting their right to limit the exercise of private power and to dispose of private property.

There can be no turning back, for two reasons. The first is that in democratic countries all major parties now accept the necessity of state intervention to direct the economy toward the achievement of social goals. There is no longer serious opposition to the concept of the welfare state which seeks, however imperfectly, to guarantee to every citizen work, education, health care, and a minimum income. There is no objection in principle to taxes on income and capital which are designed, however unsuccessfully, to redistribute wealth. The right of public agencies to regulate private business is generally accepted. Intervention by the state is often intended to prop up the business system – the government, as Karl Marx would say, acting as the executive committee of the bourgeoisie. Nevertheless, the growing power of the state and the range and ambition of its intervention are changing the nature of an economic system that is supposed to rest on private property, responsibility, and initiative. In his book *Business Civilization in Decline,* Robert L. Heilbroner says: "Perhaps the historian of the future will need some new term to depict the impending state of affairs. More likely, I think, he will simply describe it as the era of planned capitalism – the era of transition between the still business-dominated system of our age and the state-dominated system of the future."

The fundamental changes in our system are also described by Daniel Bell in his most recent book, *The Cultural Contradictions of Capitalism:*

> In historical retrospect, bourgeois society had a double source, and a double fate. The one current was a Puritan, Whig capitalism, in which the emphasis was not just on economic activity but on the formation of character (sobriety, probity, work as a calling). The other was secular Hobbesianism, a radical individualism which saw man as unlimited in his appetite, which was restrained in politics by a sovereign but ran fully free in economics and culture. The two impulses have always lived in uneasy tandem. Over time, those relations dissolved. As we have seen, in the United States the Puritan emphasis degenerated into a crabbed, small-town mentality, emphasizing only the idea of respectability. The secular Hobbesianism fed the mainsprings of modernity, the ravenous hunger for unlimited experience. The Whig view of history as open and progressive has faltered, if not disappeared, under the appearance of new bureaucratic apparatuses which have eclipsed the liberal view of societal self-management. The faiths which sustained all these beliefs have been shattered.

If it is a comfort to them, capitalists can reflect that their system has been too successful to survive. It has created an affluent society which has no use for the value system that gave birth and direction to capitalism. A consumer economy that depends on impulse buying of luxury goods on easy credit cannot claim to live by the code of restraint, thrift, and deferral of gratification. A society that promises increasing leisure as the compensation for unsatisfying, repetitive labour has already abandoned the Protestant work ethic. Private enterprise is not a credible slogan

14

in an economy dominated by giant corporations run by professional managers.

The second reason for the trend to collectivism is the explosion of scientific knowledge and its application to the economy, and indeed to all aspects of modern life. Technology has made impossible a society based on the decentralization of control and individual initiative and responsibility. The organization of the economy is now so complex that central planning and direction are essential. The computer is the symbol of the new society. Liberals who believe it possible to turn away from collectivism and back to the values of early capitalism are merely dreaming. Jacques Ellul explains in *The Technological Society:*

> The economy, with its enormous productive capacity, volume of trade, mobilization of society, and economic techniques which thirst to be applied, is no longer a closed circle, a single activity among others. It engages the life of the whole society and of all men in it. Economic problems are now the problems of the whole of society. The relation between the economy and all other human activities can no longer be merely empirical. Liberalism sufficed for the economy of a century and a half ago. Today it has no meaning.

The "impossibility of conservatism in our era" is explained by George Grant in *Lament for a Nation:*

> When men are committed to technology, they are also committed to continual change in institutions and customs. Freedom must be the first political principle – the freedom to change any order that stands in the way of technological advance. Such a society cannot take seriously the conception of an eternal order by which human actions are measured and defined. For some individuals it remains a heavenly insurance policy. Without the conception of such an order, conservatism becomes nothing but the defence of property rights and chauvinism, attractively packaged as appeal to the past.

If we are forced to stop growth, or even to apply the brakes abruptly, by shortage of resources or by rising pollution – that is, by circumstances rather than conviction – it seems probable that only powerful and centralized government will be able to impose rationing and the other necessary controls.

15

The defeat of social democratic governments in many parts of the world, the confusion evident in liberal parties, and the resurgence of what are said to be conservative parties, are no doubt reactions against the trend toward collectivism. But reactions will not reverse the trend. No matter what the political stripe of the party in power in Canada or elsewhere, it will have to respond to the same economic and social imperatives. Indeed, much of our present confusion arises from the attempt to impose the fundamentally socialist value system accepted by all parties on a capitalist system of production.

The vital question about the future has been asked by Michael Harrington in his book, *Socialism:* "One need not any longer ask whether the future is going to be collective – if we do not blow ourselves to smithereens, that issue has been settled by a technology of such complex interdependence that it demands conscious regulation and control. The question is, what form will twenty-first century collectivism take? Will it be a totalitarian, a bureaucratic or a democratic collectivism?" Given this choice, we must choose democratic collectivism, since, while we recognize that government will play an increasingly powerful role, we want to ensure it will be servant rather than master, freely elected by the people, and subject to dismissal when it ceases to respond to the will of the people.

THE NEW DEMOCRACY

Once this direction is chosen, however, we must face the fact that so far democracy has worked only in societies in which the role of the state is quite limited and where the economy is under private ownership and control. Problems have already been encountered in trying to make democracy work in the more centralized society that has emerged in recent years.

In common with other industrial democracies, Canada enjoyed a remarkable surge of democratic activity during the 1960s. The clamour to participate in decision-making was matched by the confident assumption that government, rationally managed, could solve all problems and create a just society. Affluence was to be shared and poverty abolished. The grievances of French Canadians, Indians, Eskimos and other minorities were to be redressed. Women were to be liberated.

The poorer provinces were to have a fairer share of economic development. Canadian culture was to bloom, the environment was to be cleansed, cities planned, jobs enriched, education enlightened, and even sex improved. It was an exciting decade; all seemed possible, and much was in fact achieved. But when expectations are so high, frustration is inevitable. Optimism gave way to pessimism, the politics of joy to the politics of resentment and recrimination. As the U.S. political scientist, Samuel Huntington, has put it, the democratic surge of the sixties produced the distemper of the seventies.

While Huntington was interpreting trends in the United States, Michel Crozier, a French sociologist, studied events in Western Europe; and Joji Watanuki, a Japanese sociologist, examined the state of affairs in his own country. All three were working under the auspices of the Trilateral Commission, a non-government organization linking business leaders and others in North America, Western Europe, and Japan. Their reports, published in 1975 under the title *The Crisis of Democracy,* concluded there was widespread dissatisfaction and lack of confidence in democratic institutions, raising questions about whether democracies were becoming ungovernable:

The incorporation of substantial elements of the population into the middle classes has escalated their expectations and aspirations, thereby causing a more intense reaction if these are not met in reality. Broadened political participation has increased the demands on government. Widespread material well-being has caused a substantial portion of the population, particularly among the young and the "intellectual" professional classes, to adopt new life-styles, and new social-political values. Internationally, confrontation has given way to detente, with a resulting relaxation of constraints within societies and of the impetus to collaborate among societies. There has been a substantial relative decline in American military and economic power, and a major absolute decline in American willingness to assume the burdens of leadership. And most recently, the temporary slowdown in economic growth has threatened the expectations created by previous growth, while still leaving existent the "post bourgeois" values which it engendered among the youth and intellectuals.

The diagnosis applied at least in part to Canada, but when the Canadian section of the Trilateral Commission organized a conference of academics, politicians, civil servants, journalists, and others in Montreal in May 1975 to discuss the problem of governability, a rather different attitude emerged. While conceding some problems, the Canadians reached a consensus that "governability itself may be less of a problem than 'the reality of participation,' the 'accountability of governors,' or as one participant put it, 'the democratizability of governments.' " In plainer words, the trouble with democracy lay not in the demand to participate and get results, but in the failure of governments to respond effectively to the democratic demands. In any event, said the Canadians, things weren't as bad in Canada as they were in the United States. But that optimism probably reflected no more than the usual lag in communications that ensures that problems, like fashions, reach Canada some time after they have excited the United States.

Katherine Rowcliffe, a student at Carleton University's School of Journalism, interviewed, in early 1976, a dozen opinion leaders about governability and detected a significant change of attitude. "A year's experience with inflation, wage and price controls, spending restraints, etc., has made some Canadian opinion-leaders less optimistic about Canada's ability to deal with the increasing number and complexity of problems in a democratic way," she wrote in a research report. "Most of them have serious doubts about the future of democracy. Only a few continue to be optimistic." She found MPs, journalists, academics, and others concerned about the credibility of Parliament, worried that democracy might not be able to survive if the economy stopped growing and it became necessary to reduce the income of some groups in order to meet the legitimate needs of others, and generally alarmed by the growth of the bureaucracy and the complexity of government.

When Grant Maxwell, of the Social Affairs Office of the Canadian Catholic Conference, travelled across the country in 1974 and 1975 to talk to 750 average citizens and community leaders, he noted two widely held ideas:

From the Atlantic to the Pacific, Canadians are fascinated with what is happening to one-quarter of humanity under Maoist Marxism. While there are some dissenting voices, many Canadians once fearful of anything Communist now seem inclined to give the benefit of the doubt to the Chinese experiment – at least for the present. Concurrently across Canada I heard people insisting that "small is beautiful" and that "local action is where it's at." Nation-wide there is deeply-felt disenchantment, and often an angry impatience, concerning bigness in all institutions – big governments and big bureaucracies, big corporations and big trade unions, factory-like schools and colleges, and with 'organized' religion on any scale.

Maxwell sought to reconcile the conflict between interest in the Chinese mass society and dislike for massive institutions at home by suggesting both instincts are appropriate in the ideal citizen who is supposed to have a global outlook and local involvement. A more credible interpretation, perhaps, is that Canadians who felt threatened by the growth and collision of public and private institutions over which they have no control, were looking to China in the hope it would provide a model of a more orderly and purposeful society. They were probably seeking leadership and a clear set of values rather than blue uniforms, little red books and a place in the rice paddy commune. But the public mood is not reassuring for those who believe the task is to reconcile unavoidably big institutions with democracy.

Business recession, high unemployment, the energy crisis, and the continuing problem of inflation have lately combined to dampen expectations and thus to reduce pressures on democratic governments. In an article in *Trialogue,* a bulletin published by the Trilateral Commission in spring 1976, Huntington noted with approval the reduction in both public expectations and political promise-making in the United States and in Europe. He thought that Gerald Ford was restoring the stature of the U.S. presidency and the credibility of government, and that the new Democratic Party leaders were becoming more responsible in their fiscal policies; that is, they were not promising as many expensive new government programs to solve social problems. Britain and other European countries also enjoyed, if only briefly, the spirit of hope and confidence which usually accompanies a new leader. In Canada, Pierre Trudeau clung to office, but where he had once been the personification of the surging sixties, he now became the spokesman for the sombre seventies. The change did little to restore political confidence, but it did lower expectations.

But if the problem of governability has been reduced, it has not been solved. A lowering of public demand and expectation and a loss of confidence in the political process, leading to apathy, may make it easier to govern for the time being. But as the economy recovers, we must expect and hope for a new surge of democracy. As Ralph Dahrendorf, director of the London School of Economics, remarked when he opened a conference on the Crisis of Democracy:

> They [democracies] have to avoid the belief that a little more unemployment, a little less education, a little more deliberate discipline, and a little less freedom of expression would make the world a better place, in which it is possible to govern effectively. Indeed, I think this attempt to turn back the wheels of history to try to recreate the state which we have fortunately and deliberately left is in many ways as uncivilized, indeed primitive, as the belief that all we need is nationalized ownership, public planning and worker control. Either of these mistakes must be avoided if we hope to manage to create democratic conditions which offer the largest number the largest chance for their lives.

The vital importance of strengthening our existing democratic institutions and of broadening our concept of democracy to cover activities now usually considered private is the theme of this book. If we fail to make democracy work in the collectivist new society, the alternative will not be a retreat to a former society, but some form of authoritarian government, either of the right wing or the left.

2

Parliament

Most Canadians never think to question our democratic political institutions. Are we not governed according to our constitution, the British North America Act, which enshrines the immutable wisdom of the Fathers of Confederation? Is not our parliamentary system of government clearly superior to all others?

The answer to these questions is no. The BNA Act has given rise to a form of government the Fathers would not recognize. The evidence of its shortcomings is not merely the attack of democratic distemper already discussed, but the fact we have had to invent a new system of national government based on federal-provincial negotiation. This new system has no warrant in the BNA Act, and yet for many important national issues it has replaced Parliament as the forum for debate and decision-making. The result is overlapping authority, political confusion, and frustration of the democratic process.

Let us first examine Parliament, which is supposed to be the symbol and safeguard of our freedom. The Fathers of Confederation, although they were forced to take some account of the federal nature of the country they were creating, stuck as faithfully as possible to the British model of parliamentary government. A century ago, political power was reserved for the aristocracy and the middle classes, and government under their control played only a limited role in society. In such a society, the parliamentary system may have had considerable merit, but it leaves much to be desired today, in our more fluid and democratic society, where there is a much wider demand to participate in government, and where, because government plays a far more important role in affairs, it is much bigger and much busier.

Although there have been, in both Britain and Canada, many attempts to adapt the style and substance of the system to the new circumstances, its shortcomings are being increasingly noticed and criticized. In Britain, some critics are even suggesting that the failure of the system to produce a national consensus on which policy can be based leads to instability, frequent changes of direction, and eventually to the social and economic problems that put the future of the country in grave doubt. "Britain's system of choosing governments is breaking down," wrote Joe Rogaly, a London journalist, in his 1976 book, *Parliament for the People*. "It does not produce Parliaments or policies that reflect the will of the people as a whole. It no longer guarantees the emergence of strong, widely-respected Cabinets. It is damaging our democracy, making a country that is difficult to govern almost impossible to govern. The system is out of tune with the times."

In Canada, another journalist, Walter Stewart, wrote a book about the 1972 election, *Divide and Con, Canadian Politics at Work*, in which he discovered that the popular vote was not reflected in the election of MPs. "The parliamentary result was a fraud on the people," he declared indignantly. Approaching the issue from another direction, Professor Roman R. March of McMaster University laboriously analysed the careers of some 3,000 MPs who have sat in Ottawa since 1867 to discover what must be obvious to even a casual student of Parliament: the rise of mass parties has changed not only the type of men who win election to the Commons, but the fundamental nature of the institution. "What we see today is an illusion, a mere play-acting, a shadow of its former self," said March in his book *The Myth of Parliament*.

Not many MPs accept March's view that the rise of parties has brought about a decline of democracy, but they do know that there is something badly wrong with the system. "Are we getting to the stage where democracy, a parliamentary democracy as we understand it, is really losing its effectiveness?" Bruce Phillips,

22

CTV bureau chief in Ottawa, asked Prime Minister Trudeau in an interview at the close of 1975. Phillips, a long-time observer of Parliament, went on to explain: "I would say, except as a barometer of public opinion, it has pretty well collapsed in terms of all its functions. It is virtually useless as a forum for policy formation. Parliament doesn't form policy, Cabinet does. The enormous explosion of the bureaucracy and expenditure seems to me to have far exceeded Parliament's capacity to analyse and criticize with any particular effectiveness, and when you came out with your program of controls [on incomes and profits], although I think you'd spoken all over the country many scores of times, you never made a speech in Parliament on the subject. What does that tell us about the effectiveness of the House of Commons?" The Prime Minister replied: "I think it's rather accurate and perhaps sad reflection on the House of Commons. It is becoming less and less relevant." Trudeau suggested the problem lay in the reluctance of the Opposition parties to accept changes in the rules to speed up business. Stanley Knowles, the veteran NDP member and revered authority on parliamentary procedure and tradition, has said: "The biggest problem facing Parliament is the use of its time. Its workload has multiplied hundreds if not thousands of times, but a year still has only twelve months." Knowles gave his views to a Commons committee studying reform of the rules in 1975. The last major changes were made in 1968 when the Trudeau government persuaded a rather reluctant Opposition to agree to shift scrutiny of the spending estimates and some debate on the details of legislation out of the full House into committees. "Sending more work to committees has proven to be very successful, especially with respect to legislation," said Knowles, although he suggested minor changes to restore to the full Commons scrutiny of some estimates.

The fact remains that the 1968 reforms have not speeded up the work of the House. There has been more discussion on legislation and estimates, which is of course desirable, but the rate at which bills have passed Parliament is still slower than it was a century ago despite the fact that the responsibilities of government have vastly increased. Robert M. Jackson and Michael A. Atkinson, in their book, *The Canadian Legislative System*, measured the productivity of parliaments since Confederation by calculating the number of bills passed per sitting day. Research clearly shows, they said, that Parliament has been working longer to achieve less in the twentieth century than it did in the nineteenth century. And the situation is not improving; the Commons took more time over legislation in 1968-72, after the Trudeau reforms, than it had in the period 1945-52. The average number of pages of legislation passed per day in 1968-72 was exactly the same as in 1953-57. This makes nonsense of the charge that Trudeau has stifled Parliament, but it also shows that even major and controversial changes in the rules have not solved Parliament's time problems.

Nothing that the Trudeau government or Knowles or other Opposition experts have suggested recently in the way of changes in the rules would be likely to have a major impact on the Commons. A more realistic diagnosis has been provided by John Reid, a popular Liberal backbencher who gained a perspective on the problem while serving as parliamentary secretary to the government leader in the Commons:

> In many respects what makes the House of Commons impotent is nothing more nor less than those of us who make up its membership. We have been unwilling and unprepared to give up the mythology about this place that so many of us have had bred into us when we enter this chamber. We have been unable to face the fact that the House of Commons is no longer equipped to do the kind of work that it did 100, 200, 300 years ago. . . . We have a swiftly moving society in which changes take place rapidly. Yet we in the House of Commons are profligate with our time. We do not budget our time or attempt to distinguish between what is important and what is not important. We waste our time with trivia and do not focus on the larger issues of our day.

Confirmation of this verdict is to be found in what is absent from the press almost every day: reporting of parliamentary debate. The reason is that little that is new or interesting or important is being said. "Debate has become shrill, repetitive, and increasingly remote, and irrelevant for those most concerned, the Canadian people," said the veteran Tory member and former House leader, Gerald Baldwin, in 1975. Most political journalists agree and therefore focus on the daily theatre of the Question Period, which provides lively newscopy, but also illustrates much of what is wrong with Parliament – the excessive partisanship that tends to trivialize politics.

UNREPRESENTATIVE GOVERNMENT

Having established that there are problems with our Parliament, let us approach the subject in a more organized way, starting at the beginning, which is the system of election. In each constituency there are usually three or more candidates, and the winner is the one who obtains the most votes, and not necessarily a majority of votes cast. In fact, most MPs are elected by a minority of voters in their constituency. In the Commons, the party with the largest number of MPs usually forms the government, although it often does not have a majority of all seats. The result is that we almost never have a government that has a majority in terms of votes cast at an election. We have instead a government for which most of the people have not voted.

In 1968, when Trudeaumania supposedly swept the Liberals to a great victory, they actually had the support of only 34 per cent of Canadians eligible to vote. Of those who did vote (and those who didn't bother were perhaps expressing some sort of political opinion), 45 per cent chose the Liberals. This meant that 55 per cent of voters would have preferred a prime minister and a government of a different stripe. In 1972, the government was returned by 29 per cent of those eligible to vote, and 38 per cent of the actual vote. In 1974, the Liberals won 30 per cent of the eligible voters, 43 per cent of the actual vote, and 53 per cent of the seats in the Commons.

The results are even stranger when examined on a provincial basis. In Quebec in 1974, the Conservatives won 21 per cent of the votes, but only 4 per cent (three out of 74) of the seats, whereas the Social Credit party won fewer votes (17 per cent) and more seats (11). In Alberta, the Liberals won a respectable 25 per cent of the vote, but not a single seat; the Conservatives had 61 per cent of the votes and all 19 seats.

The system is particularly hard on minor parties, which may win votes all across the country and roll up a substantial national

25

total, but win only a few seats. In 1974, the NDP got 15 per cent of the votes, but only 6 per cent (16) of the seats in the Commons. This feature of the system used to be regarded as something of a virtue. Minor parties, it was said, split the vote, divided Commons, made stable majority government unlikely, and therefore should be discouraged. The fact is that in both Canada and Britain, third and fourth parties are firmly established despite the system and must be accepted and treated fairly. Since 1957 in Canada, there have been five minority governments and only three majority governments. Instead of elections every four or five years, we have had eight in nineteen years.

Another criticism of the electoral system is that it does not reflect the realities of our politics. It requires voters to elect a local MP when their interest is actually focused on a national leader. It is sometimes alleged that television has created leadership or personality politics and thereby distorted our system, but this is not the case. Leaders were at least as important as parties long before TV became a major factor in election campaigning. John A. Macdonald ran under the slogan, "The old flag, the old party, the old leader." When his hair turned white, Wilfrid Laurier invited the voters to "follow my white plume." Mackenzie King advised that it was "King or Chaos," and in 1957 the Conservative party suddenly became the Diefenbaker party. In any event, the news media now report elections as a contest between leaders – yet only the handful of Canadians in their home ridings can actually vote for the leaders. The rest of us have to vote for surrogates – the leader's candidate in our riding. Parliament has tacitly acknowledged that voters may not even know the name of the surrogate by allowing party affiliations to be printed on the ballot. This means that voters can choose a leader by voting for his party without ever knowing the name of their MP.

Now suppose we were designing a new electoral system and somebody proposed a scheme that would not reflect the wishes of the majority, would not produce stable government, and would not permit people to vote for the leader with whom they identify. We should say such a designer was crazy, and he would be. Yet that is how our present system works. There are plenty of better systems available. According to Rogaly, only three other countries among the leading democracies elect legislators as we do: Britain, which is no advertisement; New Zealand, which is a much smaller and more homogeneous community, and the United States which elects senators and congressmen as we elect our MPs, but elects separately a head of government. This is no place to review the variety of different systems used in other democracies, but they usually ensure at least that individual legislators are chosen by a majority of voters in a riding, or that seats in the legislature are awarded in direct proportion to the votes cast for each party. In some cases electors are allowed to vote for all candidates in order of preference, so that if the first choice runs poorly, the vote is transferred to the second choice, and so on until one candidate has a clear majority. (It's interesting, incidentally, that when our politicians are choosing a new party leader, they don't award the job to the winner on the first ballot, but hold a series of ballots until one candidate has a majority over all others.)

Whatever system we might choose or invent, if it elected a House of Commons more truly representative of the will of the people, it would surely enhance the legitimacy of Parliament and government. If it reflected more accurately the division of opinion within provinces, it might also reduce strains within the country by showing that our politics are less regional and divisive than now appears. Under a system of proportional representation by province, for example, Liberals would not dominate Quebec, and Conservatives would not dominate Alberta. Having obtained 21 per cent of the Quebec vote in 1974, Progressive Conservatives would have won sixteen seats instead of three. In Alberta, Liberals would have received five seats instead of none. The NDP would have won seats in almost all provinces instead of in only five, and would thus be seen as more of a national and less of a regional party.

CLOSED GOVERNMENT

Whatever may be thought of the electoral system, there will surely be widespread agreement that parliamentary government, as it has evolved, is far too authoritarian and secretive for modern democratic tastes. The roots of the problem lie at the very roots of parliamentary system. At its beginnings in Britain, it was

27

a council representing the Estates of the Realm – Lords Spiritual, Lords Temporal, and later Commoners – called together to advise the monarch on the exercise of absolute executive authority derived from God. Eventually Parliament wrested authority from the Crown and entrusted it to an executive committee, or Cabinet, under the leadership of a prime minister. But the principle has remained until this day that the Cabinet, governing in the name of the Crown, exercises all the executive authority, whereas Parliament merely advises and gives consent.

"The government makes the decisions and all we can say is yes or no," said Knowles, defining the tradition of parliamentary government in the Commons on June 2, 1975. Ministers meet in private to decide their policies so that they can present a united front in presenting them to Parliament. Having accepted collective responsibility for their policies, they swear an oath not to divulge what passes between them so that differences of opinion remain private. The ministers command a civil service of officials who also take an oath of secrecy and owe allegiance to the minister in charge of their department rather than to Parliament. The original balance in this system of tight and private executive control was that ministers were responsible to Parliament for their conduct of affairs. If Parliament voted no-confidence in a Cabinet, or defeated a major Cabinet policy proposal, the ministers would resign to be replaced by others – or they might seek an election as a way of appealing to the voters to decide who was right, Parliament or Cabinet. This system of responsible government worked well enough as long as MPs were able to exercise more or less independent judgement. But with the rise of the modern mass political party in the last century, members began to lose their freedom of opinion and vote. It became increasingly difficult to win election without the ideological endorsement and organizational support of a party. In return, MPs pledged their votes in Parliament to the party.

Organized and disciplined national parties hardly existed at the time of Confederation. Whether the first Canadian MPs called themselves Independents or acknowledged a party allegiance, they enjoyed a high degree of independence when they voted in the Commons. In fact, about a third of the members of the first Parliament in 1867 were what Professor March, in *The Myth of*

Parliament, calls "notables" – members of established political, church, military, and legal families and other prominent citizens. Some of them were acclaimed rather than elected and owed no debts to party or leader. The first prime minister, Macdonald, complained about these "loose fish" who escaped the party net and sometimes defeated his policies. But as the parties became better organized, they learnt how to maintain discipline. The prime minister, who is also the party leader, can reward loyalty by promotion to Cabinet and punish disloyalty by leaving a member to vegetate on the backbenches. Ministers control the gift of government jobs and contracts in a member's riding. In extreme cases, the prime minister and the party can refuse to endorse a member at an election and virtually assure his defeat.

There are great advantages to the party system. It enables a party of politicians agreed upon an ideology or a policy to put a program before the electorate with some assurance that if they secure a majority, they will be able to carry it into legislation. Voters are enabled to make a choice among programs offered. But as Richard Crossman, the late British politician and journalist, wrote in 1963 in a famous foreword to Walter Bagehot's classic study of parliamentary government, *The English Constitution:* "Parliamentary control becomes a fiction with the disappearance of that solid centre of independent and independent-minded Members." Cabinets continue to exercise executive powers, but, as long as they are supported by a disciplined majority, they are not really responsible to Parliament. Parliamentary government has become Cabinet government.

There are some authorities who argue that Cabinet government has now become prime ministerial government. Certainly, prime ministers have become more important in the scheme of things in this century. Where once they were said to be "first among equals" in a Cabinet, they are now seen to dominate their Cabinets and to exercise enormous personal power.

A prime minister is head of a party as well as of a government, chosen in Canada by a national convention of party members, which sets him apart from and above his colleagues. He is the principal target for the Opposition in the Commons and for the media critics, and his popularity, or lack of it, determines victory or defeat for the government at elections. He can ask the Governor General to call an election when the moment serves him, and will be refused only in exceptional circumstances. He appoints ministers, parliamentary secretaries, and top civil servants. He has a large private staff in the Prime Minister's Office to look after his political affairs, and a large staff of civil servants in the Privy Council Office to provide him with an overview of the administration enjoyed by no other minister.

There are, of course, constraints on a prime minister. Although he may sometimes be a "majority of one" in the Cabinet, over-riding all opposition, he does depend in the final analysis on the support of his colleagues. A significant revolt within the Cabinet may bring down a prime minister; John Diefenbaker was fatally weakened by the defection of several ministers over defence policy in 1963. Although a prime minister can normally rely on the obedience of backbenchers in the Commons, he has to face their criticism at meetings of the parliamentary caucus, and persistent failure to respond would eventually weaken his position. It is important to note, however, that this opposition to the power of the prime minister occurs in private, and ministers and back-benchers usually take pains to prevent their differences from becoming known to the Opposition parties and the voters for fear of appearing weak and divided. In public, unity is the watchword and loyalty is the code of conduct.

If a major change were made in the electoral system to intro-duce some form of proportional representation, the powers of the prime minister and the Cabinet would probably be reduced since it would be unlikely that any party would win a majority in the Commons. Deprived of a disciplined majority, the government would have to seek the support of one or more of the minor par-ties. Proportional representation would make minority govern-ments the norm, and the major parties would have to accustom themselves to working with minor parties in formal coalitions organized to carry through an agreed program. This would curb the power of prime ministers by forcing them to attend to the needs of minorities; they would be subject to some extent to the independent judgement of MPs over whom they had no party con-trol. If one coalition of parties broke up, it might be possible to form another government – with or without a change of prime minister – without the necessity of an election. We might then be able to return to having general elections every four or five years instead of every time a Cabinet loses a vote of confidence or a prime minister sees an opportunity to best his opponents.

There is no reason to suppose, or experience to suggest, that coalition governments would be less decisive than single-party governments in presenting and passing legislation. In fact, the partners in a coalition would have to be agreed upon a program before forming a government, and with more parties on the government side of the House, there would be less on the Opposition side to delay passage of bills. As noted earlier, there have been five minority governments during the past twenty years, and some observers suggest they have performed better than majority governments because they have had to be more responsive to criticism.

No reform of the electoral system or change in the rules of procedure will, however, change the fact that in the parliamentary system the power to make policy is held by a small, powerful executive, operating in private, and accountable, if at all, only after the exercise of its authority. To complain about the secrecy of government, therefore, is to complain about the parliamentary system. To complain that the Cabinet makes policy with little input from Parliament is to complain about the parliamentary system. The system can be amended to make it a little more open, and this in fact is being done. For example, Information Canada was a well-intentioned experiment that failed because it was poorly planned and unfairly criticized by the Opposition parties and the press. But this was followed by a government undertaking to make available to Parliament documents demanded by MPs, except those falling within reserved categories. The categories were criticized as being far too wide, and the issue was referred to a Senate-Commons committee where the outcome seems likely to be a bill guaranteeing freedom of information within specified limits. The bill will owe much to Gerald Baldwin, the Conservative campaigner against excessive secrecy, but also something to D. F. Wall, a security expert in the Privy Council Office, who examined complaints about secrecy and concluded that many of them were valid. His internal report to the Cabinet Secretary was made public – a good sign in itself – and included a graphic example of one aspect of the problem:

"For most meetings of the Cabinet, each minister is provided with, on average, ten pounds of documentation related to the agenda. In most cases, the public information emerging from the meeting could be weighed in ounces, if not in grams." In other words, the civil service, reinforced by outside consultants, may labour to brief ministers on a problem and the policy options, but very little of this information becomes available to parliamentary critics and the public. Obviously, more information can, should, and almost certainly will be declassified and made public in future. But Cabinet will continue to control the policy-making process, insisting on the privacy of its own deliberations and on the confidential relationship between ministers and civil servants.

The great expansion of parliamentary committees in recent years has enabled MPs to examine policy issues, legislation, and administration in a more informal, less partisan atmosphere than is possible in the Commons. But the Cabinet still controls a majority of members on most committees and, through its majority in the Commons, can ensure rejection of committee reports that it finds unacceptable. The political subservience of committees is illustrated by the fact that the Commons never refers to committees matters of hot controversy and wide interest that touch upon the integrity of the government. The Opposition parties routinely demand an enquiry by a judge or a special commission outside Parliament and independent of the Cabinet. When the government agrees to an investigation, the usual course is to appoint a judicial commission, bypassing Parliament.

The inability of committees to impose policy on the Cabinet or investigate matters that the Cabinet would rather keep private has led to much frustration and to demands that committees should operate more on the lines of committees of the U.S. Congress. Conservative leader, Joe Clark, for example, has urged that committees should be free to initiate their own investigations, instead of operating only on a reference from the Commons where the Cabinet has firm control. But to give committees independent power would be to divide the powers of government. Being deprived of some of its authority, Cabinet could no longer be held solely responsible for the conduct of public affairs. This would represent a fundamental shift with far-reaching consequences unforeseen by most of those who lightly propose to enlarge the powers of committees.

IMPOTENT OPPOSITION

The concentration of executive power in the Cabinet leaves little opportunity for Opposition members to play a constructive role in the governing of the country. It is an exaggeration to say, in the words of the old British dictum, that it is the duty of the Opposition to oppose everything, support nothing, and defeat the government as often as possible. Opposition members can and sometimes do offer helpful criticism and amendments to legislation, particularly in committees when the prestige of the Cabinet is not at stake on every vote. It remains true, however, that the Opposition's major role is to discredit the government, both the ministers individually and their policies collectively. Rather than participating in government, the Opposition seeks to prevent the Cabinet from governing effectively.

The most important forum for the daily battle between government and Opposition is the Question Period in the House of Commons. There are occasions when the Question Period brings to light information a minister would rather conceal, or forces a minister to account for actions he would rather not try to explain. The knowledge that they may face interrogation also deters ministers, no doubt, from doing things they ought not to do. But even the leader of the Opposition is seldom allowed to follow up his original query with more than two or three supplementaries, and lesser political lights usually get in only one; thus, the Question Period does not lend itself to exploration of major issues, or even to a satisfying exchange of accusation and defence. Opposition members must seek to simplify complicated issues or settle for flashy accusations, and ministers often respond by withholding information or confusing the subject with obscure answers. The basic purpose on both sides is to score partisan debating points and the result is to trivialize political debate.

The political truth about the Question Period has been stated plainly by John Diefenbaker in his memoirs *One Canada:* "That one never asks a question unless he knows the answer is basic to parliamentary questioning.... A question which can be answered without prejudice to the government is not a fit question to ask, unless there is some kind of political alliance between the questioner and the government." Major issues can, of course, be taken up in debate, but debates are poorly attended by members – the Commons is almost empty much of the time – and poorly reported by the news media because the important decisions have been made in advance in the Cabinet. A minister steering a bill through the House may accept minor amendments from the Opposition, or from his own backbench supporters, but defeat of the bill is unthinkable, since it is supported by the government's disciplined majority.

In theory, the Opposition can also seek to check the government's power by holding the purse strings – that is, by scrutinizing its spending programs. This was the original power that Parliament exercised over the Crown. When the monarch asked Parliament to levy taxes to supply money, usually to fight a war, Parliament replied, "No supply without the redress of grievances." The Cabinet still submits its spending estimates to the Commons every year and MPs use the occasion to examine both policies and administration. The procedural reforms in 1968, however, provided that although the Opposition parties can scrutinize and vote against spending they disapprove of, they cannot hold up approval beyond a certain date. If grievances have not been redressed and supply voted by that date on the parliamentary calendar, the estimates are nevertheless approved by the government's majority.

Diefenbaker and other traditionalists lament what they consider to be the loss of Parliament's historic power of the purse. But the truth is that parliamentarians have neither the time, nor the expertise, nor the inclination to exercise any real control over spending, which is now in excess of $40 billion a year. As Knowles pointed out during the 1975 debate on procedure: "Some decades ago we did a fairly good job of questioning those items [in the Blue Book of estimates] dollar by dollar. But the fact is – and nobody is to blame for this – that the operation had grown so large that it became impossible to continue to deal with all the estimates here on the floor of the House." So, in 1968, estimates were referred to specialized committees, several of which could sit at one time. More days than ever were spent on scrutinizing spending but, said Knowles, MPs sitting, for example, on a committee on agriculture or on social affairs were often more concerned to improve government programs than to curb them. "So we are really not getting a study of estimates with a view to checking or limiting expenses. . . . With all the good will in the world and all the impartiality we can muster, we have not yet found a satisfactory way of controlling expenditures in any ongoing sense."

There appears to be a trend of opinion toward the view that the auditor general, who already monitors all government departments to ensure that spending is within the authority provided by Parliament, should also report on the cost-effectiveness of programs, perhaps working in collaboration with the government's own management experts. In any event, it seems the public will have to rely in future more on the auditor general for control of the purse strings and less on informed MPs.

The impotence of the Opposition in the modern Parliament leads to political frustration and disillusionment. Members who come to Ottawa, not as part-time amateurs but as full-time professional politicians anxious to contribute to the government of their country, find themselves excluded from decision-making and reduced to petty partisanship which has little appeal for today's sophisticated citizens. It is discouraging to listen to the comments of school children who have been brought to the capital to see Parliament at work and then exposed to mindless demonstrations during the Question Period or to an empty chamber during what passes for debate. The case can be made, in fact, that however satisfactory the adversary system of parliamentary democracy might have been in earlier times, when both the issues and the people were less sophisticated, it is unsatisfactory in today's complex world.

Parliament was designed to limit the exercise of power; in modern society the trend is to entrust increasing powers to government, and the need is not for a system that frustrates its employment, but for one that ensures that it is used effectively in the public interest. In Parliament, government and Opposition face each other two-swords' lengths apart (the traditional distance between the front benches at Westminster) and seek to represent the black-and-white of an argument that an educated electorate knows very well to be grey. Parliament seeks not to unite the nation, but to divide it, to base policy not upon consensus, but on sharp division.

Such criticism of the adversary system is not to suggest a one-party democracy, or a so-called democracy in which opposition is allowed only limited freedom. The United States, for example, operates an effective democracy based on division of the powers of government between the executive and legislature. The president and the Congress are not adversaries in the sense that one is government and the other Opposition; they share power and responsibility for the conduct of the country's business. The president is elected to represent the national interest; but in order to legislate he must find a majority in the Senate, which is elected to represent the States of the Union, and in the House of Representatives, which is elected on the basis of population. The Congress may also initiate legislation, but it needs the signature of the president to become law. The president has wide executive authority, but it is subject to some extent to the advice and consent of the Congress, which may even, as Richard Nixon discovered, force a president from office if he exceeds his authority. At election time, it is not enough for a legislator to report that he opposed the government; as a member of the legislative branch of government, he has to show why he supported some measures and opposed others in the interest of his constituents. Party discipline, therefore, can't be nearly as strong as it is in the parliamentary system.

There are, of course, many flaws in the U.S. system, but at its best, it promotes open decision-making by politicians seeking consensus rather than division. By contrast, the parliamentary system as we know it insists upon private decision-making and encourages divisive debate and criticism by an Opposition that is irresponsible in the sense that it bears no responsibility for the conduct of the nation's business.

SENATE AND GOVERNOR GENERAL

We cannot leave this discussion of parliamentary government without taking note of those two curious institutions, the Senate and the office of governor general.

The Fathers of Confederation had two clear purposes in mind when they created the Senate, but neither has worked out in practice. The first purpose was to assure the Maritime provinces and French Canadians that their interests would not be swamped in the House of Commons where representation was to be by population and where they would be minorities. It was provided, therefore, that each of the three regions entering Confederation – Ontario, Quebec, and the Maritimes – would have equal representation (24 members each) in the Senate, which would have power to defeat Commons legislation. It was "the very essence of the compact," said George Brown, one of the Fathers, during the Confederation debates (and quoted in *The Unreformed Senate of Canada,* by Robert A. Mackay). "Our Lower Canadian friends have agreed to give us representation by population in the Lower House, on the express condition that they could have equality in the Upper House. On no other condition could we have advanced a step." But there was a flaw in the plan, by accident or perhaps by design of the crafty John A. Macdonald, who was anxious not to dilute the power of the federal government. Instead of being elected, senators were to be appointed upon the recommendation of the federal prime minister. The result over time was that senators ceased to be true representatives of the regions, and owed allegiance instead to their patron, the head of the national government. Nowadays, the Senate is widely, if unfairly, regarded as a depository for the prime minister's political hacks.

The Fathers' second intention for the Senate was that it would check what they feared might be the dangerously democratic ideas of the Commons. "The weak point in democratic institutions is the leaving of all power in the hands of the popular element," said George Etienne Cartier. "We run the risk of being swallowed up by the spirit of universal democracy that prevails in the United States," agreed D'Arcy McGee. Macdonald was perfectly frank: "The rights of the minority must be protected, and the rich are always fewer in number than the poor." The Upper House, he said, would be "the representative of property," and it was provided that only British subjects above the age of thirty and owning substantial property could be appointed senators. These qualifications mean much less now than they did in 1867, but it remains a fact that many senators are substantial men of business, and although it is popular to accuse them of a conflict of interest when they consider and vote on legislation concerning business, they are merely performing one of the roles originally assigned to the Upper House.

Popular opinion about democracy and the rights of property have changed faster than the Senate, however, and the Upper House, now lacking both purpose and public respect, does not have the political legitimacy to challenge seriously the decisions of the Lower House. Its most useful role is that of a sort of permanent royal commission sponsoring committee investigations into such important matters as the persistence of poverty, the failure of science policy, and the state of the mass media. It should be added that during federal-provincial negotiations on the constitution in the 1960s, Prime Minister Trudeau suggested restoring some purpose to the Senate by enabling the provinces to nominate up to half the members of the Upper House so that they might again become spokesmen for the regions. The provincial premiers were not interested, however, preferring to represent their own interests rather than to appoint senators who might become rival spokesmen. The idea lapsed, and although various plans for modest modernizing of the Senate have since been suggested unofficially, it is hard to see what can usefully be done without major and more important changes in other parts of the system of government.

The British Crown was at the peak of its prestige at the time of Confederation, but with the decline of Britain and the abolition of monarchies in most other democracies, it has lost much of its mystery and majesty, and survives more for sentimental than practical reasons. The office of governor general of Canada has fared even worse; at best it reflected the glory of the British monarch, but now it glitters not at all. Attempts to give the post a new dimension by appointing Canadians to it have not had much success. Young Canadians neither know nor care who occupies Rideau Hall, nor is there any reason why they should. In 1865 Walter Bagehot pointed out in *The English Constitution* that the Crown was a useful device in Britain, but unnecessary in Canada. He argued that the British working classes were quite unfit to rule themselves; if the reader doubted that, he had only to talk to his servants! The masses were prepared, however, to entrust the country to the monarch and the aristocrats who passed in dazzling array before them. The power of the Crown was, of course, a fiction, concealing the fact that the middle class was really governing the country through Parliament and the Cabinet, said Bagehot. Such a deceit would not be required or perhaps even possible in a more enlightened country: "Where there is no honest poverty, where education is diffused and political intelligence is common, it is easy for the mass of people to elect a fair legislature. The idea is roughly realized in the North American colonies of England, and in the whole free States of the Union."

Now, more than a century after that was written, Canadians have yet to learn that they do not need a pale copy of an archaic British political device. And, even if a monarch can still serve Britons as a symbol of stability in times of change and set standards of behaviour, that role is not open to a governor general who lacks the power to attract the interest of the people.

As with the other parliamentary institutions, nothing protects the office of the governor general but tradition. Behind the familiar and reassuring façade of the Parliament buildings in Ottawa lie an unfair system of election, an inefficient legislature, an autocratic and secretive executive, a frustrated Opposition, and a couple of reminders of our colonial and undemocratic past. We can and must devise a better system of government if we hope to preserve democracy.

3

The Constitution

The defects of the British North America Act have been thoroughly documented in recent years, and the need for radical reform or even a wholly new constitution has been widely discussed. Both Lester Pearson and Pierre Trudeau recognized the failings inherent in the present situation, but despite all the concern and discussion about the Constitution of the past ten years, little has been achieved. But does it matter? Many Canadians, including politicians, seem to think the subject is only of dusty academic interest and that we can get along quite well in a practical way without concerning ourselves with what the BNA Act actually says.

They are wrong for several reasons. The first reason has to do with symbols, and was well stated by a special joint committee of the Senate and Commons that examined the Act and travelled across the country to hear public opinion:

> The purpose of a constitution is to distribute the powers of government according to the wishes of a particular national community and to enunciate its fundamental values and common goals. A constitution ought thus to be both an inspiration and a mirror of its community. Of these two ends, its inspirational role is the more important. A community that is unable to justify its existence to itself will eventually find it cannot survive by structure alone.

The failure of the attempts to rewrite the BNA Act have, in fact, revealed the basic lack of unity of purpose underlying Confederation. Instead of becoming more united, the country is becoming less united. The committee went on to indicate another reason why the constitution is important:

> A constitution may not be contained entirely, or even largely, in a written document or documents. It is not essential that it should be. What is essential is that a people should understand, accept, and even love their form of government. Without the understanding of its people a constitution is meaningless. Without their affection it is dead.

Canadians cannot understand, let alone love, their form of government, because it is nowhere adequately described, and the politicians who are supposed to manage it argue constantly over which should have the power and responsibility to tackle the problems that most concern the people. It is important, however, to examine the problem with care.

HISTORICAL CONFUSION

The roots of the problem lie in the period 1864 to 1867 when Confederation was being negotiated by delegates from Ontario, Quebec, and the Maritimes. Macdonald and some of the other Fathers wished to copy the British form of government, entrusting all authority to a strong central government. They found, however, that Quebec insisted upon reserving a measure of provincial authority to protect its language and culture, and that the Maritime provinces also had laws and customs they wished to retain. The solution would have to be a federal system of government, but Macdonald and others were reluctant. Although they recognized the inevitability of federalism, said Donald Creighton, the great authority on the period, "they could not help regarding it as a suspect and sinister form of government," because in the United States it had apparently resulted in a frightful civil war. Creighton went on in his book, *Canada's First Century*: "The 'federal principle,' as British North Americans called it then, was usually regarded as a highly potent political drug, which might prove efficacious in the cure of certain constitutions, but which must be administered in small doses, with great precautions and never without a readily available antidote."

The antidote prescribed in the BNA Act was a very strong central government with power to supervise the weak provinces. In Macdonald's phrase, "all the great subjects of legislation" were entrusted to the central government, whereas the provinces received "only such powers as may be required for local purposes." In addition, the central government could disallow provincial legislation and had undefined but broad emergency powers to ensure "peace, order, and good government." In short, Canada was to be almost a unitary state thinly disguised as a federation.

The scheme began to unravel shortly after Confederation when the provinces, led by Ontario, fought to increase their powers at the expense of the federal government and won several important test cases before the final authority on the Constitution, the Judicial Committee of the Privy Council in Britain. The judges interpreted provincial powers much more generously than Macdonald had intended. The tug of war between Ottawa and the provinces continued through the first century of Confederation, with first one side and then the other gaining ground.

About 1960, two major trends combined to give advantage to the provinces. The first and most dramatic was the Quiet Revolution in Quebec that encouraged a succession of premiers – Jean Lesage, a Liberal; Daniel Johnston and Jean-Jacques Bertrand, of the Union Nationale; and Robert Bourassa, a Liberal – to demand from Ottawa a high degree of provincial autonomy in order to protect the French language and culture.

The second, less obvious, but perhaps more important trend was the growing demand in English-speaking Canada for services that fell under provincial rather than federal jurisdiction. Education, health and welfare, highways, urban planning, and local economic development were not matters for much expenditure at the time of Confederation, but a century later they were subjects of paramount concern to most Canadians and required investment of huge sums of tax money. The provincial governments grew rapidly to meet these needs, acquiring the public support and the political and administrative muscle to confront the federal government. They demanded the freedom to manage their own jurisdiction without federal interference, and a larger share of the national income to support their programs.

To try to meet the ferment in Quebec, Prime Minister Pearson appointed the Royal Commission on Bilingualism and Biculturalism, which recommended the wider use of French in the federal jurisdiction, under legal guarantees, and the encouragement of French in provincial jurisdictions, wherever a reasonable demand existed. This concept of a bilingual Canada went far beyond the BNA Act. To meet the demand for greater provincial powers and tax revenues, Pearson proposed "co-operative federalism," which involved frequent federal-provincial conferences at every level to co-ordinate policies, an idea that would have startled the Fathers. By 1968, Pearson had concluded that even more fundamental change was required, and he left to his successor, Trudeau, the task of completing the process of constitutional reform.

Trudeau sought to entrench a Bill of Rights, including language rights, in the Constitution and failed. He sought also to work out a new division of powers in the important area of social policy where the cultural concern of Quebec and the tax concern of the English-speaking provinces were concentrated; he failed there also. There is no profit in attempting to allocate blame. Trudeau might have been more flexible. Quebec might have been more conciliatory. Ontario might have been more enthusiastic about bilingualism. The west might have been more understanding of Quebec's aspirations and more energetic in seeking constitutional change. But all were caught in the confusion created by the ambiguity of the original Confederation pact.

There was no basic agreement on what Canada should be about or how it should be governed, partly because the Fathers had left no statement of purpose, no myth to which all Canadians could automatically subscribe, and although the division of powers in the BNA Act had been amended several times, it remained at best obscure, at worst a mere historical curiosity.

The Senate-Commons Committee indicted the BNA Act in these terms:

The measure of the inadequacy of the British North America Act is that it does not serve Canadians fully as either a mirror of ourselves or as an inspirational ideal. As enacted in 1867, it

43

did not attempt explicitly to set forth any values or goals of that time except to adopt "a Constitution similar in principle to that of the United Kingdom." Whatever values it recognizes are implicit in that statement or have to be inferred from the governmental structure and the division of powers it establishes. Even the distribution of powers between the Imperial and Canadian governments and between the Federal and Provincial governments does not reflect the Canadian reality of today: an independent, democratic, officially bilingual, multicultural federal state.

The committee pointed out that sections of the Act enabling the British Parliament to amend Canada's Constitution would, if implemented, make a mockery of Canadian independence, whereas others, such as the federal power to disallow provincial legislation, had fallen into disuse. A more practical difficulty is that the Act carefully sets out the responsibilities of the two levels of government, but makes no mention of many current concerns – social services, for example – because the Fathers had never heard of them. If, as is sometimes said, the power to tax is the power to govern, the Act merely confuses the relationship between federal and provincial governments. It gives the provinces power to impose direct taxes, which, in 1867, meant mainly the property tax but which now include personal and corporate income taxes which are the major sources of revenue. The Act also gives to Ottawa the power to raise money by any mode or system of taxation, which includes income taxes. The Senate-Commons Committee summed up:

> The principal general criticisms we have heard of the present division of powers are the following:
>   (1) The Federal Parliament does not have sufficient power to manage and plan the economy.
>   (2) The Federal Parliament does not have sufficient power to cope with large multinational corporations, international unions, and the overwhelming influence and power of the United States of America.
>   (3) The citizens of Canada are handicapped by the lack of national standards in education.
>   (4) The Federal Parliament does not have the power to

implement a policy of bilingualism in education and other areas now under Provincial jurisdiction, despite the requirement of national unity.

(5) The citizens of Canada are handicapped by varying Provincial standards in fields which cross Provincial boundaries – e.g., pollution, securities regulation, labour legislation, traffic regulation, etc.

(6) The present Federal role in social legislation (particularly in shared cost programs) interferes with or prevents the Provinces from varying them in accordance with Provincial needs, resources, and priorities. It also leads to poor allocation of public funds and an excessive bureaucracy.

(7) The Province of Quebec does not feel that it has sufficient powers to guarantee the survival of the French language and culture, and to establish the social and economic institutions necessary to attain this goal. . . ."

The Committee proposed to clarify lines of power and responsibility by adopting the general principle: "A new Canadian Constitution should be based on functional considerations, which would lead to greater decentralization of governmental powers in all areas touching on culture and social policy, and to greater centralization in powers which have important economic effects at the national level."

FEDERAL-PROVINCIAL CONFLICT

There is a fatal contradiction in the committee's design. In order to provide more social and cultural services to their peoples, the provincial governments need a large and ever-increasing share of the national revenues. But in order to do its job of managing the national economy, the federal government must be able to regulate the lion's share of those revenues. The committee's proposal, therefore, would increase competition between the two levels of government, rather than encourage co-operation and rational allocation of resources.

Federal-provincial finances are already so complicated they almost defy understanding, let alone explanation. The federal government taxes to raise huge sums of money which it then transfers to the provinces to spend, sometimes in the form of conditional grants to support certain programs, and sometimes in unconditional grants that can be spent as the provinces please. In other instances, Ottawa transfers tax points; that is, it reduces its level of tax so that a province can raise its rate without the taxpayer feeling any pain. The size of federal transfers of all kinds has been rising very rapidly in recent years, and the result is that the provinces and the municipalities under their control have become bigger spenders than Ottawa. After allowing for transfers, the federal share of the total spending dropped from 53 per cent in 1950 to 41.5 per cent in 1975, whereas the provincial-municipal share climbed from 47 per cent to 58.5 per cent.

The federal government has been trying for several years to restrain the rate of growth in its transfers, whereas provinces want more money and want it without strings attached so that they can spend it as they think best in light of their own priorities. As they have grown in size and responsibilities, the provincial governments have also acquired highly capable civil servants with the expertise to match that of the mandarins in Ottawa, and they do not hesitate to question federal economic leadership.

Ontario has several times made it clear that, when it thinks that the federal government is following the wrong tax policy for the state of the economy, it will operate countervailing policies. For example, when Ottawa was squeezing the economy to fight inflation in 1971, Ontario Treasurer Darcy McKeough announced at a federal-provincial conference that his government would fight unemployment by stimulating the economy. At a conference of finance ministers in 1973, Ontario Treasurer John White tabled a brief that argued at length that the province had a far better record than the federal government in forecasting and managing the economy. The point is not whether the Ontario treasurers were right or wrong, but that they denied federal leadership in managing the economy and had the taxing and spending muscle to impose their own policies in the industrial heartland of Canada.

A further complication arose in 1975 when the federal government felt itself compelled to impose controls on incomes and profits to restrain prices. When some labour unions challenged Ottawa's constitutional right to take such action, the issue was referred to the Supreme Court. The federal government claimed jurisdiction under its reserve authority to take emergency steps to preserve peace, order, and good government. It argued that the threat of run-away inflation was an emergency and the court agreed. But this seems to mean only that the federal government can impose controls in times of emergency.

In short, it appears that the federal government is losing its exclusive grip on fiscal and monetary policies (the provinces are also becoming big borrowers at home and abroad) and lacks the power to operate an incomes policy except in an emergency.

If the Senate-Commons Committee was naive to suggest that economic power could be centralized in federal hands, it was right in suggesting decentralization of power over cultural and social policies. Ottawa launched most of the great social-security schemes, such as hospital insurance, medicare, and the Canada Assistance Plan, by offering to pay half the cost of provincially administered programs that met its criteria. This was not, however, an efficient way to manage the services. The federal government found itself committed to pay 50 per cent of whatever the provinces might spend and became alarmed by the rapidly rising costs. The provinces found their own priorities distorted by the need to put up a dollar of their own to obtain a matching dollar from Ottawa. Because neither level of government was paying the full cost, there was a tendency to extravagance. Under recent agreements, the provinces will assume full responsibility for the established programs, with financial support from Ottawa – a significant decentralization.

The provinces have also become less willing to accept federal leadership in new areas of social policy. For example, a federal proposal to make a new attack on poverty and to rationalize the jumble of welfare schemes, by introducing a guaranteed-income program on a limited basis, stalled in 1976 after three years of federal-provincial negotiations. The failure of the federal initiative reflected in part the increasing confidence of the provinces and their desire to set their own social priorities. The new affluence of the west, for example, has given it a sense of pride and identity which is often expressed in irritation with Ottawa and a determination to develop its own regional values and lifestyle.

BILINGUALISM

The west's attitude mirrors Quebec's traditional demand for control of social and cultural policy in order to preserve its language and culture. Trudeau's answer to Quebec's demand for a "special status" within Confederation was the promise of bilingualism. Instead of giving more power to the Quebec government to protect French, he proposed to guarantee the rights of French Canadians across Canada wherever a realistic demand existed. He implemented this policy in the federal sphere by passing the Official Languages Act and by spending huge sums to teach French to civil servants (although the Commissioner of Official Languages reported there had been only modest success by 1975 and suggested that resources might be better used in teaching French in the schools). In his first speech to the new Parliament in 1974, Trudeau reaffirmed his commitment to the concept of bilingualism, but lamented the slow progress and warned bleakly: "I solemnly believe that if we do not and cannot make the right [of French Canadians to communicate with the federal government and work in the civil service in their own language] a reality during the life of this Parliament . . . then it will never be done, and separatism will have proved its point and Canadian unity will cease to have meaning for the majority of Quebeckers."

But, as the Senate-Commons Committee pointed out, whatever success bilingualism might have in the federal jurisdiction, Trudeau lacked the constitutional power to impose it on the provinces, and it was here that the policy suffered its worst setbacks. Although the provinces had reluctantly accepted bilingualism as a key to national unity, they appeared to lose interest after the failure of the constitutional conference in 1971 to entrench language rights in the BNA Act. Ontario made progress in promoting French only slowly and quietly. In the west, there was said to be a popular backlash against French and the remaining French-speaking communities were gradually being assimilated by the English-speaking society. Even more serious was the fact that Quebec appeared to be retreating from bilingualism to French unilingualism.

It is doubtful if bilingualism could ever have dissolved the tensions between English- and French-speaking Canadians, as

Trudeau had promised. But the failure to reform the Constitution to guarantee language rights, and thus to compel the provinces to help protect minorities, certainly weakened the drive for national unity.

Without the language rights which might have made them more secure within Confederation, more at home in other parts of Canada, Quebeckers concentrated on their traditional demand for more provincial autonomy. Having obtained by administrative arrangements some of the authority to vary the federal family-allowance program which Trudeau had denied him at the 1971 constitutional talks, Premier Bourassa went on to ask for control over manpower programs, immigration, and communications. He also began to sound almost like a separatist. In an article in the French newspaper *Le Monde,* he said: "Quebec has set itself the ambition of being and remaining a French state within the Canadian common market." Trudeau replied indirectly by saying in a speech in Montreal: "At one time there was talk of Quebec having a special status, but fortunately that is now a dead issue. Now there is talk of a Canadian common market and of a French state within it. . . . But Canada is more than a common market." His confident statement was soon challenged by the victory of the Parti Quebecois in the 1976 election on a platform proposing political sovereignty for Quebec in some form of common market association with Canada. The new government promised to ask the consent of Quebeckers by means of a referendum before separating from Canada, and Trudeau among many others thought the voters would say no. But the case for fundamental changes in Confederation was clearly stronger than it had been before the PQ victory.

CO-OPERATION AND COMPETITION

As we have seen, the British North America Act fails to divide powers and responsibilities between the two levels of government, confuses the allocation of tax sources, and lacks a statement of language rights which all the major parties believe to be fundamental to national unity. In the absence of a workable constitution, the federal and provincial governments have entered into literally hundreds of agreements to share responsibilities and resources. Some have been negotiated and freely accepted, others have been imposed by one side on the other after bitter disagreement. Although the system may be said to work in the sense that taxes are collected, programs introduced, and the country administered, there are serious drawbacks.

The network of federal-provincial arrangements is so complex that very few persons, including working politicians, understand the real structure of government. As a result, civil servants with expert knowledge probably exert undue influence, and the entire system is protected from effective criticism by outsiders. To the public, government is a puzzle beyond solution. "The average man on the street does not carry a copy of the British North America Act or the Municipal Act about in his hip pocket," remarked Ontario Premier William Davis in a 1975 speech:

> Consequently, when he perceives a need or when he wants action in some area, his tendency is to tackle the first politician he encounters – federal, provincial or municipal – and he is not concerned about constitutional niceties. He wants action, he wants results. Consequently there is, I would admit, a tendency for all governments in the service of the people to become involved in areas that are not necessarily appropriate to them.

This was an understatement. In fact, a whole new structure of government has been created in the past fifteen years to try to manage the extraordinary range of federal-provincial agreements, co-ordinate policies, and prevent overlapping. It has become normal for the prime minister and the provincial premiers to meet several times a year; and below them, there are dozens of meetings of departmental ministers and hundreds of meetings of officials. A federal-provincial secretariat has been created in Ottawa; the federal government's most senior civil servant, with the rank of associate secretary of the Cabinet, works full time on federal-provincial affairs; Ontario, Quebec, and other provinces have offices that concentrate on intergovernmental affairs. Provincial premiers negotiate not only with the federal prime minister, but among each other in national and regional conferences at which they work out the positions they will take in Ottawa.

Trudeau, although often described as an arrogant centralist who ignores legitimate provincial claims and rights, has in fact gone to unprecedented lengths to consult the provinces. After doing very badly in the west in the 1972 election, he ordered an intensive review of federal policies of concern to the west. But instead of submitting his new proposals to Parliament, he took them and half his Cabinet to Calgary in 1973 for a formal discussion with the four western premiers. Although federal policies were involved, his action implied the provincial premiers were more important than the west's federal MPs. When the so-called energy crisis struck in 1973, he decided to fix the price of oil across Canada, and also to reduce exports to the United States. As this would have major implications for the oil-producing provinces, particularly Alberta, it was obviously right to negotiate with them. But Trudeau went beyond that to call a conference of all the provinces to try to agree on a price for oil. In the first round of negotiations, Ontario, Quebec, and the other oil-consuming provinces allied themselves with the federal government to pressure Alberta and Saskatchewan into accepting, very reluctantly, a price well below the world-market level. But when that agreement ran out, and the federal government joined with the producing provinces in saying it was time for a price rise, Ontario and others refused consent and froze prices temporarily. From the shambles of federal-provincial negotiation emerged the clear lesson that if Ottawa wanted to ensure a uniform national price, it would have to rely on the national Parliament to legislate, as the Fathers had clearly intended.

Involving the provinces in national policy-making not only diminishes the importance of Parliament, which is required only to rubber-stamp deals already made with the premiers, but gives the premiers an exalted idea of their own role. Premier Peter Lougheed of Alberta announced at one stage of the dispute over oil policy that he was breaking off relations with the federal government, as if he were the head of an independent country. The general attitude was exemplified by Premier William Davis' statement at a press conference in 1975: "The Government of Ontario cannot stand idly by while the Government of Canada plucks the Ontario taxpayers and consumers in order to feather its own nest." He was claiming the right and duty to protect the people of Ontario against a federal policy with which he happened to disagree, ignoring the fact that the people of Ontario elect federal MPs to express their judgement on federal policies. Davis' remark attracted little or no comment, illustrating the breadth of confusion about the roles of the two levels of government. Having encouraged this sort of confusion, Trudeau later expressed concern about the spirit of independence manifest in the provinces. Having defeated Quebec's claim for special status, he claimed in a CTV interview at the end of 1975 that he was encountering the same problem elsewhere: "You've seen more and more provinces that think they should have a special status. You know, just a couple of years ago it was Alberta and Saskatchewan [presumably he was referring to the oil-price crisis]. For a time we thought it was Ontario before the election [presumably a reference to the militant position of the Ontario Government concerning taxes and oil prices before the provincial election in 1975]."

Another result of federal-provincial duplication is to encourage bureaucracy and waste money. "Do we really need eleven Departments of Labour in this country?" asked William Davis in his 1975 speech. "Must both levels of government promote trade overseas? And so the list goes on. I believe we owe it to our people and we owe it to each other to find means of improving the situation quickly. And by improving the situation let me state categorically that I do not mean elaborate new intergovernmental machinery and further bureaucratic burgeoning. I believe we have seen enough of that and indeed my objective is to simplify and not to complicate." Davis went on to say he believed powers and responsibilities could be rationalized without fundamental constitutional change, but added: "I am convinced that the long-run health of our Confederation, our economy, and our country depends on rationalizing our division of responsibilities between Ottawa and the provinces."

Another effect of constitutional confusion is a weakening of the democratic process. It becomes increasingly difficult for governments to accept responsibility and act decisively; increasingly attractive for politicians to avoid responsibility by passing the buck; increasingly hard for the citizen to perform his duty of following events so that he is able at election time to reward those politicians who do well and punish those who fail.

TOWARD REFORM

The case for a new constitution is clear and has been widely acknowledged – although there is no such agreement on what the constitution should say or on how it should resolve the fundamental problem of federal-provincial conflicts. It seems clear, however, that if the new society is to be governable by democratic means, we shall have to make radical changes in our institutions, or construct new ones. (If this disturbs conservatives, they should consider that the choice may be between evolution and revolution and that the urgent need for reform of Parliament and overhaul of the Constitution has been widely accepted by the most respectable authorities.) The question, therefore, is how the changes and reforms are to be made and who is to take the initiative.

The unhappy experience with the federal-provincial constitutional conferences in the period 1968-71 offered the lesson that politicians in power are too busy to devote sufficient time to a consideration of reforms and, in any event, have too much invested in the existing system to be anxious to make many changes. They have not even been able to agree, at the time of writing, on a formula for bringing the BNA Act from Britain to Canada, let alone on any changes that might be made in that archaic document.

What is needed now is a political leader with the imagination to win election on the promise to convene a constitutional convention (as Diefenbaker once suggested). The convention might well include representatives nominated by all the "Estates" of the modern realm: the two Houses of Parliament and the provincial legislatures; the municipalities; the national political parties; business, agriculture, and labour; the professions and learned societies of academics. Such an assembly could invite the widest public participation and attract enormous public interest, and its conclusions would no doubt have to be submitted to the public in a referendum. Such an exercise in writing and adopting a new confederation pact would be a powerful influence for Canadian unity – or in the event of failure, would show that no satisfactory basis for Canadian statehood existed, because French could not be reconciled with English, or west with east, or because some other fundamental cleavage, cultural or economic, could not be bridged.

Unity would not necessarily imply centralization of power. Perhaps the opposite, for decentralization from Ottawa to the provinces in many areas of administration seems not only inevitable but desirable. A trend toward decentralization of power appears to be emerging in other industrial democracies with different political systems, and the truth may be that our Constitution and structure of government are in a mess because they are out of step with historical development in highly developed countries.

In the United States, the loss of confidence in central government is such that in the 1976 election President Jimmy Carter sought popularity by running "against Washington." In Washington itself, the legislature is asserting its power over the national executive, and there is also a program to return tax revenues and programs to state and city governments. In Britain, the Mother of Parliaments is being forced to yield some jurisdiction to Scottish and Welsh assemblies. On the continent of Europe, minorities that have long been submerged in national states are claiming recognition. In Canada, it is not only French Canadians who insist upon cultural distinction, but also native peoples and immigrant ethnic minorities. Even in the United States, the famous cultural melting pot seems not to have worked as well as once was thought.

At first sight, this emphasis on local control and return to cultural roots may seem to contradict another trend apparent in industrial democracies, the rapid development of a supranational society that overrides national borders. (The growth of the supranational system is described in detail in the final chapters; it is enough for the present to say it joins the western democracies in a common economy and a common popular culture.) But perhaps the trends to localism and to supranationalism are complementary. When the people of a region within a national state begin to realize there is no longer a distinct national economy under firm national control, they turn to a government closer to home – in Canada, to a provincial government – to protect their interests. Similarly, when they begin to realize there is no longer a distinct national culture to give them identity, they turn back to earlier identities – or in a developing region such as the Canadian West, they seek to create at least a sub-culture. The national state is thus being eroded from both ends; it is losing power to the supranational system and to regional systems within its borders. How these trends will work themselves out in the long term is beyond any reasonable horizon of speculation. One can only guess that we may see the emergence of a supranational federal state in which the political units will not be the countries we now know, but provinces or even cities with distinct economic and cultural identities.

However that may be, in Canada we have to deal in the short-term with the reality of decentralization that is invalidating political institutions designed for a centralized state. There is the procedural problem that Parliament simply does not have the time to supervise the existing areas of federal jurisdiction, let alone new areas. There is the democratic problem that big governments tend to become prisoners of their bloated bureaucracies. One solution to both problems would be to devolve power from the central government to provincial governments. A provincial government could provide the same or more services than the federal government, but be smaller, more flexible, more open because it is governing fewer people and responding to fewer conflicting interest groups.

This is not to say there would not be in Ottawa a strong flag-ship government to lead the country. Strength does not equate with bigness and public respect. In fact, the image of today's federal government is flabby inefficiency. With a narrower mandate, the national government would be able to do a better job and earn more respect at home and abroad.

NOTES ON A NEW CONSTITUTION

Having attacked the parliamentary system, reviewed the shortcomings of the BNA Act, and urged the need for new institutions, I am open to the objection that it is easy to criticize, hard to propose alternatives. Paraphrasing Winston Churchill, it may be said that our present system of government is the worst possible except for all the others. On the other hand, to offer a blueprint for a new system of government is pretentious and a provocation to critics to fall upon the mistakes one is bound to make in such an undertaking. Nevertheless, I am offering an outline of a new structure of government, if only to encourage others to do better. After all, the professional politicians have tried and so far failed; it is perhaps time for the outsiders to have a go.

A Preamble
As Trudeau said in 1969 and the Senate-Commons committee repeated in 1972, a constitution ought to state the objectives of the country. Canadians might rally to a declaration embodying the following principles:

The citizens of Canada declare that their state exists to guarantee the maximum freedom of the citizen consistent with the welfare of the nation.

They agree that the freedom of the individual can be abridged in the greater interests of the nation only by laws adopted by a democratic parliament and interpreted by independent courts, as defined below.

The citizens further declare, however, that the following freedoms are fundamental and may be abridged only by a resolution carried by a majority of not less than two-thirds in both Houses of Parliament declaring an emergency to exist and specifying the fundamental freedom or freedoms to be suspended:

Freedom of thought, conscience and religion.
Freedom of opinion and expression.
Freedom of association and peaceful assembly.

The citizens of Canada recognize English and French to have been the languages of the two founding nations at the time of Confederation, and declare them to have equal status for purposes of federal, provincial, and municipal government, education, and the administration of justice, in the national capital and in those counties of the founding provinces (Ontario, Quebec, Nova Scotia and New Brunswick) in which both languages are commonly used for private and public purposes, as defined from time to time by law.

The citizens of Canada further declare that it is the right of every person to receive an income not less than half the

56

national average, and they guarantee that where it is not possible for a person to earn such an income by work, the state will make up the deficit.

In summary, this preamble would seek to establish three principles: First, that Canada is a democratic country under the rule of law in which basic liberties are guaranteed. It would recognize that there may be emergencies, such as war or insurrection, in which it is necessary to suspend freedoms, and would provide a parliamentary mechanism. The Cabinet would not be able to declare a state of emergency on its own authority, as it did for example during the FLQ crisis in October 1970. Second, it would recognize that the rights of French and English should be guaranteed for public purposes in those areas in which bilingualism is already a reality – principally in areas of Quebec and the adjoining areas of Ontario and New Brunswick. The pretence of preserving French in the west, where bilingualism appears unacceptable, would be abandoned. Third, the abolition of poverty by introduction of a minimum income program would be guaranteed. (The problem of poverty is discussed in detail in a later chapter.) This would be a basic economic right to accompany basic political and language rights.

Structure of government
To implement the undertakings in the preamble and to carry on the national business, the following structure of government is suggested.

1. The Speaker of the House of Commons to be also the Head of State for ceremonial purposes.

This would acknowledge the supremacy of Parliament and go a little way to reassure those disturbed by the disappearance of the monarchy, which has become divisive in Canada.

2. The Queen and her successors to be recognized as Head of the Commonwealth.

This would maintain sentimental tie to Britain and a diplomatic link with the Commonwealth.

3. The Prime Minister to be elected as Head of Government by a direct national vote.

This would conform with the political reality that voters identify with a national party leader and vote for him, in effect, rather than for a local MP.

4. Prime ministerial election to be open to the leader of any party which won 10 per cent of the national vote in the previous general election to the House of Commons. In the event of more than two candidates running, voters to be required to indicate on their ballot their order of preference for each candidate. If no candidate had more than 50 per cent of first preferences, the candidate with the lowest number of votes to be eliminated and the second preferences of his or her supporters distributed, and so on until one candidate had a clear majority of votes.

This would eliminate crank candidates and ensure the Prime Minister would be elected with a genuine national mandate.

5. The Prime Minister, the runner-up (to be known as the Leader of the Opposition), and any other candidate obtaining more than 10 per cent of the vote to be members-at-large of the House of Commons.

This would ensure party leaders a seat in Parliament without the necessity of facing another election, or having the distraction of a constituency to service.

6. The House of Commons to be elected by proportional representation.

A number of different systems are available and merit study. But it would probably be best to elect MPs in constituencies as at present, and then to achieve the appropriate level of party representation from each province by appointing additional members from lists provided by the parties. It is unlikely that any party would win a majority of seats in the Commons, and the Prime Minister, with the authority of his national mandate, would have to organize and lead a coalition.

7. The Prime Minister to select his cabinet from members of the Commons, and to attend the House with his ministers not less than once a week for an unlimited Question Period.

8. The Prime Minister to hold office for five years, subject to death, resignation, or dismissal by a formal vote of two-thirds of the members of the Commons. In the event of a vacancy, the Speaker to offer the House the option of inviting the Leader of the Opposition to become Prime Minister, or holding a general election.

It will be noted that simple defeat of a government bill or proposal would not force the resignation of the prime minister. He could accept defeat, reshuffle his coalition, or resign if he thought the rebuff sufficiently serious. He could be removed only by a substantial majority of MPs. On the other hand, he would not have the power, as he does at present, of calling an election more or less at whim, to get the better of his opponents.

9. The provinces to choose their own form of democratic election and government.

This would continue, more or less, the present situation in which provinces can amend their own constitutions.

10. The Senate, or Upper House of Parliament, to be composed of the Prime Minister and nineteen members of his Cabinet; the Leaders of the Opposition parties in the Commons and their nominated supporters to a total of ten Opposition members; the Premier, the Finance Minister and the Leader of the Opposition from each province.

The Senate would thereby become a federal-provincial chamber of government, with thirty federal and thirty provincial members, for the purpose described below.

11. The duty of the Senate to be the management of the economy to ensure as far as possible a high level of employment, stable prices, a viable balance of international payments, the abolition of poverty, and the equitable distribution of revenues to finance a similar and adequate level of public services in all parts of the country.

The Senate to have the exclusive power to levy taxes and borrow money on the public credit for both federal and provincial purposes; the power to regulate incomes, profits and prices; and the obligation to divide resources between the two levels of government in such a way as to enable them to meet their responsibilities, as defined below.

The Senate to have under its jurisdiction a National Department of Finance, a National Department of Revenue, the Bank of Canada and the Economic Council of Canada. The official heads of these agencies to form an Expert Economic Commission for the purpose of reporting to the Senate, not less than once a quarter, on the state of the economy and recommending appropriate policies.

The Senate to invite into public consultation not less than once a year representatives of business, industry and commerce, labour, agriculture, consumers and such other interest groups as may be considered appropriate, together with representatives of municipal government, to discuss economic policy.

The Senate, composed in effect of delegates from the elected federal and provincial legislatures, would become the national economic authority, bringing the public finances and responsibility for management of the economy under unified control.

The responsibility for recommending economic policy to implement the stated goals of full employment, etc., would lie with expert advisers. It is already the case, of course, that civil service experts advise on policy in private; under the proposed arrangement, the advice would be public. The power to legislate would lie with the elected Senators, who would be required to consult in public with outside interest groups.

In the Senate, the Prime Minister and members of his Cabinet would form the largest single bloc – twenty out of sixty. But in order to legislate, they would have to win the public support and votes of their federal opponents and/or a substantial number of provincial members.

Although there would be equal numbers of federal and provincial Senators, they would represent governments and oppositions and deadlock would seem unlikely. Meeting in public with expert advice and a heavy national responsibility, the Senators would be under powerful pressure to compromise and reach at least a majority decision. However, it might be wise to provide that in the event of a tie vote, the federal Prime Minister – the only Senator with a national mandate – would have a casting vote.

In return for surrendering the power to levy their own taxes, the provinces would be guaranteed a voice and a vote in making national economic policy and fair share of national revenues. It might be necessary to write the current formula for equalizing tax revenues, or an improved version, into the constitution.

While the federal Parliament and provincial legislatures would not have the power to legislate in areas of economic policy, they would be free to debate economic issues and, if they wished, recall their delegates to the Senate by changing their government.

12. The Commons to have jurisdiction over external affairs and defence; the criminal law; regulation of trade and commerce, with authority to delegate this responsibility to provincial governments where desirable; national transportation and national communication; immigration and citizenship; postal and other national services.

There would thus be no shortage of work for the federal Cabinet and the Commons. Although they would be constrained by the spending limits imposed by the Senate, they would be responsible for the prudent use of funds allocated to them.

13. The provinces to have jurisdiction over health and social services; local government and urban development; education and the encouragement of the arts; police, the administration of justice, and the civil law; highways and other forms of transportation within the province.

The provinces would thus control those services essential for the preservation of local tradition and identity. In these areas, they would be free from federal interference, although they would be subject to spending limits imposed by the Senate. (Such an arrangement would not satisfy the Parti Quebecois, which seeks nothing less than separation, but it might appeal to moderate elements desiring more autonomy and greater recognition within a more effective federation.)

14. Disputes over the division of powers, or the allocation of powers not specified in the constitution, to be resolved by majority vote of the Senate, subject to appeal on points of law to the Supreme Court.

15. Candidates for appointment to the Supreme Court to be nominated by any Senator, approved by majority vote of the Senate, ratified by the Commons and the legislature of the province in which the candidate practised law.

16. Senate and Commons to hold a joint session not less than once every five years to consider and vote upon amendments to the constitution proposed by any ten members of either House. Amendments approved by majority vote of the Joint Session, to be recommended to the legislatures of the provinces. If approved unanimously by the legislatures, to become law. If approved by a majority of the legislatures, but not by all, to be submitted to the people in a referendum. If rejected by a majority of the legislatures, to be considered defeated.

So much for a do-it-yourself constitution. If the reader has been provoked to ask a hundred questions, raise a score of objections, think of a dozen improvements – good. Faced with an unsatisfactory form of government more than a century ago, the Fathers of Confederation got together to offer ideas, negotiate, and finally compromise on what became the BNA Act. We are just as competent to negotiate a new constitutional pact suitable for our century, seeking not eternal truths but to accommodate current political realities.

4

The Media

The mass media of news and commentary are important parts of the political and social systems. The way in which they are owned and operated will have a powerful and perhaps decisive influence on the shape of the new society.

POLITICAL POWER

The news media are the principal channel of communication between politicians and the public – the gatekeepers who regulate to a considerable extent the flow of information and opinion in a democratic society. As Conrad Winn, a specialist on communications in the political process, wrote in *Political Parties in Canada:*

> The communication system is vital to the political process because of the enormous dependence of modern man on impersonal rather than personal sources of information. Because politicians are largely inaccessible to the ordinary public, citizens are obliged to rely on newspaper, radio, and television for all kinds of political information. Even party elites depend greatly on the media. Politicians employ the media to secure information on government activity, on the performance of the economy, and on shifts in public sentiment as well as to test ideas and wage electoral warfare.

Politicians acknowledge the role of the media with both flattery and resentment. In Britain, as early as the eighteenth century, the press was described as the Fourth Estate, and more powerful than the other three estates of the realm, the Lords Spiritual, the Lords Temporal, and the House of Commons. Prime Minister W.L. Mackenzie King declared that the press gallery was an adjunct of the Canadian Parliament. The U.S. Constitution recognizes the role of the press in the scheme of democratic government by specifying that Congress may make no law abridging its freedom. On the other hand, the British Prime Minister Stanley Baldwin, outraged by the political pretensions of the press owners, said they sought prerogatives of the harlot, power without responsibility. Prime Minister Trudeau, arguing that the conventional wisdom always threatens to become a tyranny, wrote: "There is thus a danger that the mass media – to the extent that they claim to reflect public opinion – constitute a vehicle for error, if not indeed an instrument of oppression. For my part, I have never been able to read newspapers without a sense of uneasiness, especially newspapers of opinion. They follow their customers and are therefore always lagging behind reality." Presidents Lyndon Johnson and Richard Nixon came to regard the media as their most dangerous enemies, if not indeed traitors to the Republic, and Vice President Spiro Agnew damned them in a famous piece of alliteration: "Nattering nabobs of negativism."

In Canada, as in other democracies, the media have changed both in structure and style over the past quarter century. Where once we had a regional press with influential and independent papers in every province, we now have national media. The television networks carry the same news and views on national politics from coast to coast. Newspaper chains and syndicates distribute across the country the opinions and interpretations of pundits and reporters in Ottawa. *The Globe and Mail* has claimed for itself the title of Canada's national newspaper, and while its circulation is not large, its prestige is considerable. It often sets the agenda not only for other papers, but also for the politicians in Ottawa who look to it for guidance on what issues to raise that day in Parliament. *Maclean's* magazine, while always a national journal of opinion, is now seeking to become a national newsweekly, rivalling in Canada the reach and influence of *Time* and *Newsweek* in the United States. The style of political journalism has changed from reporting to interpretation and analysis. Reporters are no longer satisfied to record the facts; they now seek to put them in context, explain their significance, and suggest what impact they could – or perhaps should – have on events. It is in many ways a superior form of reporting, but it is also open to abuse and raises questions about the role of journalists in the political process.

Daniel P. Moynihan, the American intellectual, senior official under presidents Kennedy, Johnson, and Nixon, and now a senator, argued in an article in *Commentary* in 1971 that in seeking to improve itself by recruiting young reporters from the universities, the u.s. press was acquiring journalists trained in what has been called the "adversary culture." The editor of *Commentary*, Norman Podhoretz, stated the case more precisely in a note on Moynihan's theory:

It is admittedly difficult to distinguish in the abstract between a skeptical or critical attitude on the one side and an attitude of preconceived hostility on the other; between the impulse to expose dishonesty or error or corruption on the one side and the impulse to discredit through the tendentious manipulation of evidence on the other; between the wish to keep the officials who conduct the public business honest in every sense, and the wish to prove a case against the entire set of arrangements through which the public business is conducted in a polity like our own: between, in short (to borrow from the late Richard Hofstader), the realm of "socially responsible criticism" and the realm of the adversary culture. Yet difficult though it may be to draw them in theory and sometimes even in practice, such distinctions are nevertheless real and crucial and need to be drawn. In the case of the news media in general, the influence of the adversary culture shows itself not so much in the treatment of individual events – although it certainly shows itself there on a sufficient number of occasions – as in a marked disposition to seek out and play up stories which feed the belief that the country is breaking down. Not that the country has problems which it has been struggling to solve with varying degrees of failure amounting sometimes to success, but that the country as we know it is about to be defeated at last by the deficiency of its institutions and by the mediocrity and venality of its leaders.

The U.S. news media went on, nevertheless, to score their greatest victories over the elected politicians. The reporting of Vietnam formed a public opinion that forced President Johnson to retire. The reporting of the Watergate affair helped to bring down President Nixon, although a reading of those events suggests the role of the press has been exaggerated: most of the stories in the media resulted from leaks from the official investigative bodies, such as the grand jury. The reporters performed the important function of keeping the issue alive and before the public so that it could not be buried, but they turned up little in the way of original information. As *Fortune Magazine* said in its April 1975 issue, however: "These are the glory days of the American press. Never before has it exercised so much power so independently or found itself vested with such prestige and glamor." *Fortune* reflects the concerns of Big Business, but its article entitled "The New Concerns About The Press" brought up to date the issues raised earlier in *Commentary:*

> A new generation of Americans – better educated, more interested in ideas, more concerned with political and social questions – gave many institutions a more "intellectual" character in the 1960s. The influence of this new generation on the press was dramatic. It had a special impact on the new national newspapers, which began developing new journalistic forms; furthermore, the national press as a whole seemed to have a new consciousness of American society and was conveying a new and more "serious" agenda to the American people.

Although the new journalism was in some ways a great improvement over the old, said *Fortune*, it seemed to express a systematic distrust of all established institutions.

> There is growing concern among these executives [in business and government] that the new journalism has made it hard for them to make their records and views known to the public on their own terms. As examples, they point to the almost unremittingly hostile coverage received by the Pentagon and the oil

industry in recent years. The consequence, argue these executives, is that it has become increasingly difficult, if not impossible, to get the public's governmental and economic business done.

One is immediately provoked to ask why government and business should be able to present themselves on their own terms, rather than through the filter of sceptical journalists, and *Fortune* drew on the writings of the late Walter Lippmann, one of the most thoughtful and respected of U.S. journalists, to reply:

> Lippmann argued that the central transactions in a modern democracy are between its institutions, which do most of the actual work, and the publics that oversee and control them. The central role of the newspaper is to facilitate those transactions by simply reporting what happened – the one thing it can do with precision and expertise all its own. But it can perform this function properly only when it leaves to responsible institutions the task of defining events. When newspapers try to usurp that function, they cease to be a window through which publics and institutions can look at each other, and start to act as a screen. That, said Lippmann, is why "at its best, the press is a servant and guardian of institutions." When it relinquishes that role, he warned, it becomes "a means by which a few exploit social disorganization to their own ends." Some aspects of the new journalism, then, have put the system somewhat out of joint by making it more difficult for government, business, and other institutions to explain themselves to their publics. In the long run, it would seem, something will have to give: the effectiveness of government, the ability of public opinion to control it, the freedom of the press or the character of the journalism it currently practises.

There appear to be some second thoughts in the United States about the nature of reporting and the role of the press. Wes Gallagher, president and general manager of the Associated Press, the news service co-operatively owned and operated by the U.S. press, suggested in a 1975 speech to managing editors that:

> What we and the country need today might better be called "accountability reporting," instead of investigative. . . . Politi-

cians are accountable to their constituents for their actions. It is our job to make certain the constituents get accurate and timely reports. . . . Accountability reporting must be done with accuracy, not innuendo, and be in an objective, impartial tone – explanatory, not strident or accusatory.

Fortune Magazine and Gallagher were concerned that the new press was losing credibility, but if this is so, it is a very recent development. Although most institutions in modern democracies have suffered a loss of public confidence, the U.S. media have risen in public esteem, according to opinion polls. In his study of governability for the Trilateral Commission, Samuel Huntington wrote:

The most notable new source of national power in 1970, as compared to 1950, was the national media, meaning here the national TV networks, the national news magazines, and the major newspapers with national reach such as the *Washington Post* and *The New York Times*. . . . In the two most dramatic domestic policy conflicts of the Nixon Administration – the Pentagon Papers and Watergate – organs of the national media challenged and defeated the national executive. The press, indeed, brought about what no single institution or group, or combination of institutions and groups, had done previously in American history. It forced out of office a president who had been elected less than two years before by one of the largest popular democracies in American history. No future president can or will forget that fact.

In summary, it is argued in the United States that the news media have changed their role in the political process and substantially increased their influence, whether for good or ill.

Canada is not the United States. Our TV networks do not have the resources of the U.S. giants. We have no national newspapers of the stature of *The New York Times* and the *Washington Post*. We also have a different form of government. As we have noted, in the United States there is a division of powers between branches of government rather than an adversary relationship between government and opposition, and the U.S. press, protected and encouraged by the Constitution, seems to assume some of the role of an opposition. In Canada, the opposition is institutionalized in Parliament, and the primary job of the media is, or should be, to report that debate. When they adopt the U.S. idea that they are adversaries of government – that is, opponents or even enemies – they are allying themselves with one side in the debate, the opposition. Instead of being reporters, they become critics, seeking to discredit the government. This is not to say reporters have no investigative function; it is their business to find out as much as they can about the inner workings of government and indeed of the opposition parties, but they need to do so with responsibility and restraint, and not with a missionary zeal to "throw the rascals out."

We should note in passing that hostility toward government and politicians is a liberal attitude and inappropriate in a modern social democracy. It stems from the belief that government is a necessary evil that needs to be checked at every turn, its power confined, and pretensions exposed, so that free men can go about their private business with minimum interference. In a social democracy, government is not an oppressor, but a liberator; not a conspiracy against the people, but the peoples' best hope for advancing their collective welfare against private wealth; not a threat to freedom, but the means by which ordinary people can escape bondage to private power. Democratic governments do not always live up to their ideals, unfortunately, and it is the proper business of the press to report their failings. But when journalists assume it is their role to be adversaries of the government of the day simply because it is the government, they are accepting the liberal rather than the social democratic or even conservative view of society.

Most Canadian journalists would probably deny they see themselves as adversaries and argue that they are seeking only to explore the news in greater depth so as to reveal more of the truth. This is laudable, but also extremely difficult. As Lippmann pointed out long ago in his book *Public Opinion*, news and truth are not the same thing, and when the journalist seeks to go beyond recording facts,

> His version of truth is only his version . . . where there is no objective test, his own opinion is in some vital measure constructed out of his own stereotypes, according to his own code, and by the urgency of his own interest. He knows he is seeing

the world through subjective lenses. . . . The control exercised over him by the opinions of his employers and his readers is not the control of truth by prejudice, but of one opinion by another opinion that is not demonstrably less true.

There has been no Vietnam or Watergate in Canada to stimulate the adversary culture and heat the blood of adversary journalists, but some U.S. experiences and attitudes have influenced the conduct of the media. Allegations of fraud by companies obtaining federal contracts to dredge harbours were promptly labelled a "harbourgate scandal" and given sinister political connotations. Every hint of scandal involving politicians was played up as a major sensation threatening the life of the government. Revelations in the United States about the activities of the CIA were faithfully echoed in speculation by Canadian journalists about the activities of the agency here.

Canadian politicians also have expressed concern about what they believe to be the growing power of the media in the democratic process. Joe Clark, the new Conservative leader, asked what he thought about the impact of the media on the convention that chose him, replied: "It's inevitable. There's no way you can get away from it. You simply have to accommodate to it. Not only the convention; it's also the House of Commons, and I think we simply have to recognize that that is something we have to live with. . . . I don't object to their [the pundits'] influence. I am worried about the narrow base of their information." On the government side, ministers expressed in private their concern about the difficulty of conveying information through news media pre-occupied with investigative and interpretive reporting. Heward Grafftey, a Conservative MP and leadership candidate, probably reflected an opinion widely held by politicians when he said during an interview at the Conservative convention: "Louis St. Laurent told me when I first came into politics back in the fifties: '. . . this is going to be the biggest job of your generation to combine democracy with the television medium.' And he was right."

It is interesting to note also that at least some political journalists in Ottawa who move into government are critical in retrospect of their previous attitudes as reporters. Douglas Johnson, who interviewed a number of former journalists to find out why

71

they left journalism to work in government, in a research project at Carleton University School of Journalism in 1976, reported: "Many of the interviewees indicated that their experience in government had taught them how they, as journalists, would be better able to penetrate the labyrinth of government agencies and departments so as to obtain information when they wanted it. Yet at the same time, they indicated they'd be a lot less quick to use that information in a facilely critical way. Most spoke of being more 'objective or comprehending' of the problems and lapses of government departments."

In summary it seems fair to say that, although the politicization of the media in Canada has not developed to anything like the same extent as it has in the United States, journalists are playing a more aggressive and influential role in the political process.

SOCIAL POWER

In addition to their power in the political process, the media exert a more subtle but perhaps more important influence on the wider society. According to the sociologists, they preserve the ideology of a society – that is, they promote the shared values and beliefs that legitimize institutions and bind a society. "To ensure that a value system does not become so vague that it ceases to perform its social function of providing cohesion, it is necessary to build into certain social roles the task of restating and generalizing values," wrote John Porter in his pioneering examination of Canadian society, *The Vertical Mosaic.* "Individuals who have a particular facility with the written and spoken word and who can manipulate symbols assume these ideological roles. At the lower levels of social development such are the roles of the medicine man, magician, shaman, soothsayer, myth-maker, and story-teller. In the modern complex society the roles are found in the operation of the mass media, the educational system, and the churches, that is, the roles of writer, publisher, editor, teacher, clergyman, professor, and lawyer." Porter observed that although these "custodians of values and interpreters of social experience" operated at different intellectual levels and addressed different audiences, "the unifying of value themes is achieved through control of media of communication." He went on: "The ideological system must provide the justification

72

for the economic system, the political system, and so forth, and this it does by attempting to show that the existing arrangements conform with the traditional value system." One does not have to follow Porter in every detail to accept his general statement that the mass media do define what is normal and respectable in a society, what is debatable, and what is beyond discussion by decent, responsible citizens.

The report of the Special Senate Committee on the Mass Media (entitled *The Uncertain Mirror*, and popularly known as the Davey Report, after the committee chairman, Keith Davey), touched on the same idea of media power when it said:

> One of the truly depressing aspects of our inquiry was the ingenuous view of so many media owners that they are mere spectators. They're not spectators. They control the presentation of the news, and therefore have a vast and perhaps disproportionate say in how our society defines itself. . . . The power of the press, in other words, is the power of selection. Newspapers and broadcasting stations can't dictate how we think and vote on specific issues; but their influence in selecting those issues can be enormous. Of course the people won't always vote the way the editorial-writers tell them on next week's sewer bylaw; but who decides when they'll start thinking and talking about sewers – or whether they'll worry about pollution at all?

In terms both more academic and more radical, Wallace Clement, in his book *The Canadian Corporate Elite*, argued that mass media have the potential to promote the ideas of the ruling class on a scale undreamed of by, say, Karl Marx. He said: "It may be that the 'end of ideology' espoused by many defenders of the existing order in fact means the end of a prevalent ideology in opposition to the dominant ideology, thus providing a lack of contrast needed to make apparent the dominant ideology." In other words, modern media are so massive and persuasive that far from encouraging communication and debate they prevent the development of any alternative to the conventional wisdom.

IN WHOSE INTEREST?

Given that the media exercise direct influence on the political process and indirect influence on the formation of social values,

73

one has to ask in whose interest the influence is used. The traditional answer is that the media serve the public interest by creating a free market in information and ideas from which truth will emerge. Indeed, said the fathers of the free press, from John Milton in the seventeenth century, through struggles of the eighteenth and nineteenth centuries, the *only* way to establish truth was to expose all ideas, all opinions, all information to the test of public scrutiny and free debate. Lies, false rumours, and wrong ideas might have their day in the forum of public opinion, but rational men would eventually sort out the truth, and the truth would make them free. The Senate Committee took as its text a modern statement of this "libertarian" theory of the press by the American jurist, Hugo Black, in a 1944 case: "The widest possible dissemination of information from diverse and antagonistic sources is essential to the welfare of the public . . . a free press is a condition of a free society." The senators elaborated: "The more separate voices we have telling us what's going on, telling us how we're doing, telling us how we should be doing, the more effectively we can govern ourselves."

But this theory of the press was being criticized as out of date long before the Senate report. "The twentieth century . . . brought a gradual shift away from pure libertarianism, and in its place began to emerge what has been called 'the social responsibility theory of the press,' " wrote Theodore Peterson in *Four Theories of the Press*. He explained:

> The theory has this major premise: freedom carries concomitant obligations; and the press, which enjoys a privileged position under our U.S. government, is obliged to be responsible to society for carrying out certain essential functions of mass communication in contemporary society. To the extent that the press recognizes its responsibilities and makes them the basis of operational policies, the libertarian system will satisfy the needs of society. To the extent that the press does not assume its responsibilities, some other agency must see that the essential functions of mass communication are carried out.

In the United States, the Commission on Freedom of the Press in the 1940s reflected concern about the shortcomings of the media and articulated the theory of social responsibility. In Britain, the Royal Commission on the Press arose from similar concerns and ideas, and in Canada, some twenty years later, the Senate Committee ploughed much the same ground with similar results. All emphasized the danger of encouraging state control of the media and sought to encourage voluntary self-regulation. The Senate Committee, for example, said: "Canada needs a Press Council. We think government should have nothing whatever to do with its formation or operation. . . . We think many of the problems of the press that this report documents could be alleviated by the existence of a watchdog organization that would monitor the press the way the press monitors society." Press councils were established in Ontario and Quebec, as in the United States and Britain, and they have served as courts of appeal for individuals who felt the press had been unfair or inaccurate or had acted in bad taste. But the councils have had little success in dealing with the more general concern that, in ways hard to specify and document, the press is reporting the wrong things, ignoring the important trends, and presenting only conventional views. Nor for that matter have press councils, at least in Canada, grappled with the charge that the media have adopted the adversary culture and set themselves up in opposition to established institutions.

The Senate Committee briefly acknowledged some of these less tangible concerns about the media, but preferred to concentrate on a trend of events that could be described in reliable numbers: the concentration of media ownership. The senators took the view that there was likely to be a libertarian press speaking with antagonistic voices only if there were independent owners. The committee found that 77 of Canada's 116 daily papers were owned by groups or chains, and that in many communities the owners of the press also controlled radio or TV stations. "There is an apparently irresistible tendency, which the economists describe as the process of 'natural monopoly,' for the print and electronic media to merge into larger and larger units," said the report. The process has continued, at least with regard to the ownership of daily papers. Robert G. Clarke, in a research paper prepared at the Carleton School of Journalism in 1976, updated the Senate research and found 88 of 115 dailies were owned by groups. But so what? The Senate Committee, although seeking "more separate voices," could not argue that group ownership meant fewer or inferior papers. Indeed, it conceded that group management sometimes cured papers that had been ailing under independent ownership, and that the quality of a paper did not equate with its form of ownership. Some group papers were excellent, some independent papers awful. The Committee could only theorize: "If the trend toward ownership concentration is allowed to continue unabated, sooner or later it must reach the point where it collides with the public interest. The Committee believes it to be in the national interest to ensure that point is not reached." Perhaps wisely, the senators did not attempt to define the national interest, but recommended establishment of a Press Ownership Review Board with power to disallow mergers that did not appear to be in the public interest. The board, it was conceded, would have to use "criteria of a fairly subjective nature," but the intention would be to place the onus on anyone proposing to purchase a newspaper to demonstrate that, "he is in as good or better position to serve the public interest than is the present owner." As the senators had not been able to show that mergers were in fact harmful to the quality of the press, it is not surprising that the government took no action on the proposal. Mergers continued, although Clarke noted that the number of distinctly different dailies has actually increased slightly, and the general level of quality may have improved.

The Senate report probably focused too closely on newspapers and gave too little attention to the rise of other media. It complained there were only five cities in which genuine newspaper competition existed, but Canadians have access to two or three TV networks, numerous radio stations, an increasing variety of periodicals, and, of course, an extraordinary range of books dealing with current social and political issues. In short, Canadians are exposed to more voices than ever.

The question now becomes not, "How many voices are there?" but, "For whom do they speak, and what do they say?" Porter reported in *The Vertical Mosaic:* "Canada's mass media are operated as a big business. Many of them, particularly in the large cities, are closely linked with corporate enterprise." He went on to show that ownership of the mass media was closely held by a number of prominent families, and said: "A large proportion of the men who control the major newspapers belong to upper-class institutions. They are graduates of private schools and belong to the same exclusive metropolitan clubs as do members of the economic elite. Almost all of them have been to university. They all belong to the British charter group of Canadian society." Clement, in *Canadian Corporate Elite,* went further to study the links between those executives and directors who control the media and those who control the major corporations. He reported: "The overlap with the economic elite is extensive, almost one half the members are exactly the same people. Moreover, those not overlapped resemble very closely the economic elite. The conclusion must be that together the economic and media elite are simply two sides of the same upper class: between them they hold two of the key sources of power – economic and ideological – in Canadian society and form the corporate elite."

To this point, Porter and Clement were dealing in facts, give or take a definition of what constitutes an elite, but then they side-stepped into speculation. Given that the media shape the ideas and values of a society, and given that the media are controlled by members of the upper class, they assumed that the members of the upper class use the media to preserve the existing society in which they hold a privileged position. Porter said: "The ideological orientation that results from the existing pattern of ownership is conservative, supporting the status quo over a wide range of social and political and economic policy." Clement declared: "The media, through the ideology they present, reinforce the existing political and economic system. The mass media are not the pillars of capitalist society; they do, however, add important support to the structure and serve to reinforce the continuation of existing inequalities."

The theory sounds reasonable, but it is still only a theory about how the media may be expected to act, and not evidence of how they do act. Porter, in fact, seems to have modified his view since publishing *The Vertical Mosaic.* In a foreword to Clement's book, he questioned the conclusion about the media elite and asked whether capitalists own media primarily to make profits or to promote their ideology. He answered: "I suppose the test case

77

would be where capitalists continued to operate newspapers and broadcasting stations at a loss, subsidized from their other activities, to serve their ideological interest. I would think such a case difficult to find." Clement might reply, of course, that when the capitalists own all the media voices, there is no point in keeping two alive at a loss, when one will serve to maintain the ideology and make a fat profit in a monopoly situation. On the other hand, one could point out that in Britain, capitalists grew richer by publishing papers that appealed to a mass audience by supporting the Labour Party – for example, the successful *Daily Mirror*. In Canada, the *Toronto Star* became the most successful daily, in part, by supporting the labour movement when most capitalists thought unions were an invention of the devil.

Many working journalists would argue also that ownership of a paper (or a broadcasting station) does not necessarily give control over what is published (or broadcast). They would readily concede that the owner or his agent can direct opinion expressed on the editorial page, but they would insist that what appears in the news columns is determined by the professional judgement of reporters and editors, and that what appears in a signed column or a review reflects the views of the writer alone. Porter attempted to dispose of this argument with summary judgement based upon splendid scorn for the pretensions of mere journalists:

> As a group reporters have no disciplined academic training in any particular sphere, although they seem prepared to write about almost anything. They do not as an occupation group license themselves, govern their own affairs or establish their own forms of performance. As Bernard Shaw pointed out so long ago, they have no public register. As an occupational group, they are not highly paid, nor do they seem to have high prestige. Hence it is unlikely that, as a profession, journalists would have the social standing or professional expertise or group solidarity to offset ownership pressure, although occasionally, as individuals, editors can rise to great prominence.

Clement added:

> If the editors are not in fact part of the controlling family, as is often the case, they tend to be long-time employees who have

spent their entire careers with the company. In the long process before being selected by controlling interests to become an editor, they come to learn "the rules of the game" through the long socialization and selection process.

But what rules? Is it implied that owners dictate to editors, and editors pass on to reporters, a list of events that can be reported and of those that must be ignored, a list of ideas that are safe and those that must be suppressed, a list of opinions that can be given prominence and of those that must be buried in the truss ads, as we used to say when such ads ran at the back of the paper? Journalists would laugh at such an idea, but they would perhaps acknowledge that they are bound by quite a different set of rules – the rules that define what is meant by news. In an entertaining essay on "The Nature of News" in *Journalism, Communication and the Law,* Phyllis Wilson shows that news is defined and re-defined by journalists. "In the first analysis, the determinant of news is the reporter's perception of which facts, opinions, and ideas he gathers are interesting or important. On that perception, reporters often disagree, among themselves, and with their editors," she says. Nevertheless, she quotes with approval a definition by William Johnson, a member of *The Globe and Mail's* Ottawa bureau, who wrote during the 1974 election: "The mass media have their own imperatives: the news must somehow conform to the dynamics of the theatre. What is not new is not news. What is not paradoxical, dramatic, incongruous, shocking or momentous has little news value." One can add that what is new, paradoxical, dramatic, incongruous, shocking, or momentous *is* news and will be reported, whether the owner likes it or not, with very rare exceptions that tend only to prove the rule. If the owner or editor is so unwise as to seek to discipline the reporter, he will nowadays usually confront a union able and willing to defend journalistic integrity and to appeal to public opinion on whose confidence in the "freedom of the press" the owner ultimately relies for profit and influence.

This argument that journalists, rather than owners, determine what is news also draws support from the concern, described earlier, about the new journalism and the adoption of the adversary culture. Media owners may very well approve of journalists placing themselves in opposition to government, if they see government as a threat to their private power. In this context, adversary journalists are serving the interests of capital. But the owners could hardly approve when journalists become adversaries of Big Business, as *Fortune Magazine* complained that they do. If the owners could manage it, they would surely prevent the exposure of corporate scandals, or the disclosure of corrupt links between business and politics, or the reporting of speeches and opinions about corporate "rip-offs," or the encouragement of consumer causes. The fact that businessmen constantly complain about their treatment in the media is evidence that they do not in fact control the media.

We can also observe that when news media are under public control, they act in ways very similar to those under private ownership. The news values of the CBC, which is responsible to government and Parliament, are the same as those of CTV which reports to private capitalists. The explanation, at least in part, is the competitive nature of the news business; what one TV station has, its rival must match; what appears in the newspaper will be picked up by TV and radio, and vice versa.

This is not to say that the journalists' definition of news is satisfactory. It often values speed over completeness, brevity over explanation, sensation over sobriety, immediacy over perspective, conflict over co-operation, the event over the trend, the entertaining triviality over the difficult but important; and it is summed up in the saying that only bad news is good news, meaning that death, disaster, decay, and destruction make headlines, whereas normal life, success, growth, and construction are too dull to be interesting. Journalists are constrained far more by these conventions than by the ideology of owners. As John Harbron, the news analyst, has remarked, the real trouble is often that journalists lack the intellectual competence to do what they say publishers won't let them do.

A CONCLUSION

Assuming that one of the priorities in the new society will be to extend public authority over private power, it is inevitable and desirable that private ownership of the mass media of news and commentary will be sharply challenged. Indeed, in a struggle between democratic government and private privilege, it makes no sense that one side should continue to control the principal means for setting the agenda and reporting the debate, even if private control is not as complete as sometimes alleged. The Senate Committee, despite its support for private ownership of the media, advised: "We must start thinking of [news] as a public resource like electricity." Public resources are not usually left under private control, and one can turn Justice Black's libertarian dictum on its head by arguing that a privately owned press is incompatible with a democratic society.

The difficulty is to devise a better system of ownership. State control might be less desirable than private monopoly, although in fairness one has to note that the CBC operates one of the best and most impartial news services in Canada.

The solution may be to entrust ownership of the principal media of news not to government or private interests, but to public corporations representing and responsive to the community. The corporations in turn could appoint publishers and editors to be responsible for day-to-day management of the paper or broadcasting network in accordance with the highest standards of journalism.

To ensure the widest freedom of expression, media of interpretation, analysis and opinion should remain under private ownership.

If this appears to be a dangerous departure from the libertarian ideal, it is worth noting that the Canadian people seem to be seeking reform of the media, and the choice again may be between evolution and revolution. Grant Maxwell, summing up in April 1976 his report on the attitudes and aspirations of Canadians at the grassroots of society, said:

The social power of the media – TV advertising and news reporting especially – worries many Canadians. Occupying the middle ground between policy-makers and the general public, the media select, report, and interpret "the news," and sometimes also "make news." Given this immense power to inform and interpret, Canadians in many walks of life are asking a greater accountability from the media. People are asking, in effect, "Can't the media be required to be more socially responsible, and still remain free?"

PART TWO:
THE NEW ECONOMICS

5

The Economy

"The economy, the society is out of joint," said Prime Minister Trudeau in a CTV interview at the end of the turbulent year of 1975. "When you have very high unemployment and very high inflation at the same time, obviously the system is not working well." With 7.1 per cent of the labour force out of work (the highest rate since 1961) and the cost of living up almost 11 per cent in a year, most Canadians agreed. But there was little agreement on what was causing the economic problems, and the alarming statistics provoked angry recriminations and divisive arguments.

Labour leaders accused government of allowing business to rip-off consumers by charging excessive prices and making obscene profits. Business leaders accused government of excessive spending and taxing, and attacked labour for demanding excessive wage increases. When the government imposed controls on profits and incomes in an attempt to restrain prices, it was promptly accused of destroying free enterprise and free collective bargaining. The Prime Minister's mention of the need for a new society with new values provoked speculation that he was planning some form of corporate or fascist system of government, an extraordinary outburst of bitter criticism from the business community, and the threat of a general strike from the Canadian Labour Congress.

The first objective for the new society must be to get the economy back into joint. Only when the economy is under control and there is a social contract on how to divide the product will it be possible to achieve other goals of the new society. But the truth seems to be that we are at a turning point in which the old economic ideas don't work and the solution of our problems waits upon the development of new economics. If this sounds unduly dramatic, it is worth taking a brief layman's look at some of the previous turning points at which new economic ideas made possible the transformation of society.

The prevailing economic wisdom of the seventeenth century was what later became known as Mercantilism. Governments regulated trade with taxes, tariffs, subsidies, and other devices to encourage exports and discourage imports, thus increasing the flow of bullion into the country. The wealth of a nation was measured by how much gold and silver it had in the vaults.

In the eighteenth century came the industrial revolution and Adam Smith, a canny Scotsman whose book, *An Inquiry into the Wealth of Nations,* was the manifesto of the dawning age of capitalism. The true measure of a country's wealth, he said, was not its bullion, but its capacity for production. To increase production, government should scrap the laws and regulations and let businessmen go about their business of investing in new machinery and organizing workers to perform specialized tasks in mills and factories and mines. The businessmen would in turn be subject to the discipline of the free market. They would compete to produce the best goods at the lowest prices, and the consumers would reward the successful and bankrupt the failures. The market, said Smith, would also serve as an automatic economic regulator, matching production to demand. When a line of production proved to be profitable, other businessmen would rush into the market, and as supply increased, prices and profits would come down. So although businessmen would be motivated only by self-interest – the desire to make a profit – they would be "led by an invisible hand" to serve the public interest more effectively than if that had been their intention. Rising production would create demand for labour and so raise wages. Smith was right about the dynamism of free enterprise, but too optimistic about the ability of the market to maintain economic equilibrium. The economy grew through cycles of boom and bust rather than by steady expansion, and during the periods of bust, workers suffered unemployment and grinding poverty.

The suffering of the working class gave rise in the nineteenth century to the thinking of Karl Marx and other socialists who predicted that the concentration of wealth in a few hands and the increasing misery of the great majority would lead to the overthrow of capitalism. They expected the workers to seize the means of production and eliminate the private owners who were draining off part of the product of their labour in profit. They were wrong about that, at least in their own century, but by focusing attention on the defects of capitalism, they created a political pressure for reform, if not for revolution. Reform involved increasing government intervention to regulate the market and to correct its excesses by taxing wealth and subsidizing the poor.

The twentieth century brought the First World War, the first total war between industrial countries, in which governments took over the planning and direction of national economies and directed them toward national goals. Then came the Great Depression and a period of fear and confusion as governments first tried to return economies to market forces in the hope they would restore prosperity, and, when that failed, experimented with new regulatory agencies, job-creating programs, and welfare schemes.

From this crisis of capitalism emerged the New Economist, John Maynard Keynes, with a theory to explain why Adam Smith's unseen hand was not guiding the economy as predicted. The technical details of his theory need not concern us. What was important was his solution: governments should intervene to counter the natural cycle of the market. When business investment was trending down and private savings were piling up, threatening a slump, government should increase its own spending to create demand. Spending more than it took in taxes, government would have a deficit in its budget which it could cover either by borrowing the private savings not being used in the market, or by creating new money through the banking system. When the economy was on the upswing, with demand for goods and investment capital threatening to outstrip supply and force up prices, the government should tax more than it spent, tucking the surplus into savings and thus reducing demand.

Keynes also taught that it was necessary to redistribute income from rich to poor in order to keep an economy on an even course, since rich people tend to save too much rather than spending their money and creating demand for goods. Progressive taxation and social security schemes would transfer some of the money to lower-income people who would spend it and, by encouraging production, increase the general wealth. Although Keynes' *The General Theory of Employment, Interest and Money* was published in 1936 and became the new wisdom among professional economists, it was some years before it was accepted by governments.

The Canadian government was forced during the Second World War to take command of the economy and to mobilize it for war production. Planning and spending and direct controls were introduced on a scale that had been rejected as unthinkable during the Depression. They not only solved the problem of mass unemployment, but rapidly expanded the economy and stimulated it to extraordinary feats of production. At the same time, the common effort and sacrifice of the war years generated a new sense of social purpose and a determination to avoid the injustice and inefficiency of the pre-war times.

Responding to these ideals and with the confidence born of wartime experience, the government undertook to manage the economy so as to maintain full employment. The central idea was not to restrain enterprise or replace the market as the governing mechanism, but to aid and encourage the development of capitalism by correcting its defects, as Keynes had prescribed. By any reasonable standard, the new system worked marvellously, not only in Canada but in other democratic countries. The economy expanded rapidly, and the new wealth financed a rising standard of living for all – although not in equal measure, as we shall discuss later. By 1950, after eighty-three years of Confederation, the gross national product (GNP, the annual value of all the goods and services produced in Canada) had reached $33.7 billion; in the next 25 years, to 1975, it more than tripled to $109 billion (that's in "constant" dollars after discounting the effects of inflation). Disposable income jumped from less than $1,000 per person in 1950 to more than $4,500 in 1975, far outstripping the rise in prices. The number of Canadians working almost doubled, and with the aid of machinery and improved skills, their productivity increased as their hours of labour shortened. At the same time, current government expenditures soared from $4 billion in 1950 to $66 billion, making available better health, welfare, educational, and cultural services, in addition to supporting business growth.

There have, of course, been setbacks and disappointments. We have not enjoyed full employment but there has been no mass unemployment on the scale of the 1930s and of earlier depressions, and social security has relieved the suffering of the jobless. We have not enjoyed stable prices, but incomes have run ahead of inflation. We have suffered brief recessions as well as booms, but there have been no slumps of the pre-war type. In fact, the GNP has increased every year during the past quarter century. Even during the recent worldwide slowdown, which was widely regarded as the worst since the 1930s, the Canadian economy continued to grow. Those who now complain that unemployment and inflation are ruinous and that the economy is in a shambles have lost their sense of proportion. They are demanding perfection and overlooking the fact that in comparison with the past, we have been managing our affairs wonderfully.

It is not only Canada that has enjoyed this unprecedented growth. The respected British journal, *The Economist,* noted that the GNP of the world tripled in the quarter century, 1950-75. It is hard to grasp the significance of that statistic. It means that the product of human labour and ingenuity edged upwards through thousands of years of history to reach a certain level in 1950, and then was suddenly multiplied by three in the flicker of history's eye. In many countries, unfortunately, most of the increased production was consumed by increasing populations, but the truth remains that we have discovered how to manage our economies so as to bring about rapid growth. Our present problems arise not out of failure, but out of success.

THE PROBLEM

Flaws began to appear in the marvellous new machine in Canada in the mid-1960s. The economy had been underemployed in the late 1950s because Liberal and Conservative governments had failed to apply enough stimulation to offset a business recession. Growth was low and unemployment relatively high. When the Liberals regained power in 1963, recovery had already begun, but they proceeded to overstimulate the expansion. Spending began to rise rapidly, and in 1965 income tax was cut by 10 per cent at a time when expansion in the United States was already creating a strong demand for Canadian exports. "We all recognize that many of us misjudged the situation," acknowledged Bob Bryce, deputy minister of finance during those years, and a disciple of Keynes, in a paper delivered in 1970 to the Institute for Economic Research at Queen's University. The Prices and Incomes Commission, which was established in 1969 to study the cause and cure of inflation, reviewed the record and reported in 1972:

> The Canadian economy had begun its long climb out of severe recession in the spring of 1961. The subsequent rise in output and employment was sufficiently vigorous to bring about a progressive reduction in the substantial margin of slack which had developed in the economy at the turn of the decade. By the end of 1963 the seasonally adjusted national unemployment rate was back down to 5 per cent of the labour force and still declining, profit margins had risen sharply, exports were expanding rapidly and a strong upswing in capital investment spending was under way. Over the next three years the level of aggregate money expenditure in the economy surged ahead at an average rate of more than 10 per cent annually. Propelled by this stepped-up rate of demand expansion, exceptionally large gains in output and employment were experienced, carrying the seasonally adjusted national unemployment rate down to the unusually low level of 3½ per cent of the labour force by the autumn of 1965. Up to this point price and wage levels had been rising at relatively low, though gradually accelerating, rates. By the second half of 1965 this accelerating trend was becoming quite pronounced. A marked escalation of interest rate levels was also under way. In retrospect it seems clear that the pace of recovery in Canada had failed to moderate in time to permit the economy to settle on a substantial growth path compatible with reasonable stability of the price level. Instead, the country found itself caught up in a relatively severe outbreak of inflation. By 1966 prices and wages in

Canada were rising about twice as rapidly as they had been rising only two or three years earlier.

This story illustrates the inability of governments to fine-tune the economy – that is, to apply the Keynesian remedies with sufficient precision to avoid recession, on the one hand, and inflation, on the other. The swings were much less serious than they had been in pre-Keynesian times, but they were still painful.

Several factors help to explain the failure of management. One has already been discussed in a previous chapter – the refusal of provincial governments to follow the federal lead. H. Ian MacDonald, an economist who became a civil service adviser to the Ontario government and is now president of York University, confessed in a speech in Toronto in 1975:

> A number of years ago when teaching monetary and fiscal policy, I was as guilty as any of applying the unitary state of the world of Keynesian economics to the Canadian federal system. How easy it was to simply sketch in the inflationary or deflationary gap, and then swing the great levers of monetary and fiscal policy into action to exercise a counter-cyclical influence. The correct mix of monetary and fiscal policy would be sufficient to restore equilibrium in the economy. However, Canada is not a unitary state. . . . We are a federal state and a highly decentralized one, with immense economic and fiscal powers in the hands of the provinces.

He went on to cite the experience of 1970 and 1971 when Ontario deliberately applied expansionary policies to counter the federal squeeze.

Another problem complicating management of the economy is the fact that economic statistics, although much improved in quantity and quality, still do not provide a perfect picture of what is happening in time to allow government to take action. There are also time lags of up to two years between the application of fiscal and monetary policies and their full impact on the economy.

And then there are pure politics. The state of the economy is probably the single most important factor in the popularity of a government. When the economy is slowing, the Opposition has a chance to win office by promising to speed it up. There is always a powerful incentive to politicians, therefore, to avoid the correction of a slowdown and encourage demand and expansion. High unemployment was a major factor in bringing the Conservative government to the edge of defeat in 1962, setting the scene for its collapse in 1963. The Liberals came to power promising to cure unemployment and introduce expensive new social services. But after winning the 1965 election, the Liberal government became alarmed at the rate of inflation and began to try to restrain the economy. There were promises of austerity and appeals to the public to exercise restraint. When this was not sufficient, a special anti-inflationary budget was introduced in the fall of 1967 – and defeated, as it happened, when the Conservative Opposition staged a parliamentary ambush in February 1968, and caught the Liberals without enough members in the Commons to carry the bill. A slightly revised bill was introduced and carried, and by then unemployment was beginning to rise, reflecting reduced demand in the economy. Prices should have eased, but instead they continued to rise.

This was the perplexing situation that confronted Trudeau when he became prime minister in 1968. The Keynesian remedy did not seem to be working. His reaction was to intensify the measures of restraint. "The most urgent need now is to check the continuing increases in prices and living costs," said Finance Minister Edgar Benson when he introduced the Trudeau government's first budget in October 1968. He proposed to restrict spending, to freeze the size of the civil service, to raise taxes and to squeeze excess demand out of the economy. Still prices rose, and in his 1969 budget, Benson squeezed tighter. "We really mean business in the fight against inflation," he said, predicting the first surplus of taxes over spending for some years. The Bank of Canada, at the same time, drastically reduced the rate of increase in the money supply, making credit more expensive and thus discouraging both consumers and businessmen. Trudeau took to TV, urging Canadians to practise voluntary restraint; and at a press conference at the end of the year, he warned: "I'm afraid there are a lot of people who are bargaining that the government can't act tough for too long because it will only get frightened if it sees unemployment go up to 6 per cent. . . . But if people think we are going to lose our nerve because of that, they should think again because we're not." This statement, interpreted as a threat to create unemployment, was sharply criticized, not only by opponents on the left of politics, but also by Conservatives and the news media.

This criticism revealed a new factor in the situation: the opinion-leaders were no longer prepared to accept the discipline implied by Keynesian techniques. Trudeau was said to be callous, which was untrue, and to be fighting inflation on the backs of the unemployed, which was true – but was also the conventional way of dealing with the problem. Conservative leader Robert Stanfield was among many who insisted there had to be a better way to stabilize the economy, and he helped to make it a political issue by going across the country to talk to the unemployed and dramatize his concern.

The Prices and Incomes Commission confirmed later that Trudeau's orthodox actions had succeeded in squeezing excess demand out of the economy, but prices continued to rise. "What is the explanation?" asked the commission.

A good question, but before we look at some of the suggested answers, it is important to note that subsequent events have vastly confused the situation and made the problem of 1965-70, which seemed so difficult at that time, appear relatively simple.

The rate of price increase dropped in 1970 and 1971, more because of good harvests and a supermarket price war than because of the government's squeeze. Trudeau seized the opportunity, however, to make the first of several premature announcements of victory over inflation and to turn his policy to stimulation of the economy. He was in part responding to political criticism and preparing for the election of 1972 in which it was clear that unemployment would be the main issue to be exploited by the Opposition.

By encouraging expansion and employment, Trudeau and his new finance minister, John Turner, succeeded to some extent in defusing the Opposition, but even so the government won only the narrowest of victories. It faced the new Parliament with a minority of seats, dependent on the support of the NDP and racing against time to prepare for the next election by introducing popular programs. Measured in the National Accounts, which are more comprehensive than the budget, federal spending jumped an extraordinary $6 billion in 1973-74. Also in 1973, the country was hit by the international shockwaves from the enormous increase in oil prices, poor harvests which sent food prices soaring around the world, a commodity boom, and rampant inflation in the United States and other major trading countries. In the familiar cycle, bust followed boom and in 1974 and 1975, the world economy slid into the worst recession since the 1930s. Canada fared better than the United States and most other industrial countries because the government maintained domestic demand by increasing its own spending, as Keynes had prescribed.

When the world recovery began in 1975 and 1976, however, it became clear Canada had not learnt the need for restraint as well as others who had suffered more. For example, unemployment had jumped higher in the United States than in Canada, and U.S. unions appeared more prepared than Canadian unions to modify their wage demands. Wages and other incomes rose faster in Canada than in the United States, putting new pressure on costs and prices and the ability to sell Canadian goods in competitive world markets. Although the Trudeau government had won the 1974 election with a promise not to impose income and price controls, it claimed the new circumstances in 1975 justified reversing policy and imposing restraint on incomes and profits to ease pressure on costs and prices.

Through this period of roller-coaster economics, prices, profits, incomes, and unemployment all increased. Consumer prices jumped 4.8 per cent in 1972, 7.6 per cent in 1973, 10.8 per cent in 1974, and 10.8 per cent again in 1975. Only a few years previously, the government and the country had been alarmed when the rate of price increase rose above 3 per cent; now there was double-digit inflation.

Corporation profits, which had fallen sharply in 1970, rebounded to rise 12.8 per cent in 1972, 35 per cent in 1973, 27 per cent in 1974, before turning down 3 per cent in 1975. Part of the surge in profits was cyclical as the government spurred expansion, and part of it was simply the result of inflation: as world prices soared, inventories of materials held by corporations increased in value and returned superprofits when they were sold. But when the corporation restocked at the new higher prices, much of the windfall profit was absorbed in working capital. Nevertheless, the corporations had made a real gain, although it was in the nature of a one-time capital gain rather than a normal operating profit.

Wages, salaries, and supplementary labour income also advanced during the period, more steadily but less dramatically than profits: 8.4 per cent in 1970, 9.8 per cent in 1971, 11.4 per cent in 1972, 13.4 per cent in 1973, 16.8 per cent in 1974, and 14 per cent in 1975.

Through it all and in apparent defiance of Keynesian economics, unemployment was high and tending to rise: 5.9 per cent in 1970, 5.4 per cent in 1971, 6.3 per cent in 1972, 5.6 per cent in 1973, 5.4 per cent in 1974, and 7.1 per cent in 1975. To a country educated to believe that anything above 3 per cent unemployment meant widespread hardship, evoking memories of the Depression of the 1930s, unemployment at 6 and 7 per cent was profoundly alarming and evidence of bad economic management. Under considerable public and political pressure throughout 1970-74 the government stimulated the economy by spending and tax cuts to increase production and the demand for labour. But unemployment stayed high while inflation worsened.

Similar problems have afflicted the United States and other industrial democracies. Over all the developed world, the question has been raised and fiercely, sometimes bitterly, debated: What has gone wrong? Why does the market, with a little help from government, no longer regulate prices, profits, wages, and employment in a satisfactory way?

THE DEBATE

Many different answers are being suggested, but they generally fall within one of a few major schools of thought.

Big Government
Most businessmen argue with great conviction and considerable support from professional economists that the reason the market no longer works efficiently is that government interferes too much.

Government intervention takes many forms. Government agencies regulate some industries, setting prices and conditions of business. Government laws restrict some forms of competition and encourage others. Government taxes are adjusted to stimulate some types of economic activity more than others, and government spending redistributes the profits of business and the wages of labour. Government labour legislation permits workers to join unions which are, in effect, monopolies because they deny the employer the right to hire labour in a free market. Government income and profit controls currently in force are, as Trudeau has acknowledged, "a massive intervention in the decision-making power of private groups."

Government intervention of the types mentioned has generally been introduced to correct obvious defects in the market system – for example, to prevent monopolies or near-monopolies from exploiting consumers. While businessmen often criticize this sort of intervention in detail, there is not much opposition in principle.

The form of intervention that now attracts the loudest complaints is the rapid increase in government spending. Businessmen argue that, however the public spending is paid for, it adds to costs and prices. If it is paid for by taxes on profits, it becomes a direct cost to business which has to pay the taxes. When taxes are deducted from a worker's pay packet, they encourage him or her to try to get the money back by demanding higher wages. When government borrows money to cover spending, it competes with private borrowers and may force up interest rates, adding to the cost of production. When government prints new money to pay its bills, it may dilute the value of the currency. Indeed, it seems obvious that if the amount of money increases faster than the supply of things to buy, over time the value of money will decline. Businessmen argue, therefore, that if government would restrain spending, reduce taxes, and increase the supply of money only in step with the real growth of production, the market would resume the task of regulating the economy.

There is no doubt that spending by all three levels of government – federal, provincial and municipal – has increased dramatically. It rose from $4 billion in 1950 to $11 billion in 1960 to $31 billion in 1970 and $66 billion in 1975. Some of this rise simply paralleled the growth in population, the increase in production, and inflation itself. But in addition, governments have been taking and spending a larger share of the total national income. The governments' share of GNP rose from 30 per cent in 1965 to 40 per cent in 1974.

But the problem with the businessmen's analysis is that governments have intervened precisely because the market system was not satisfactory. Governments tax and spend and create money to try to make sure we do not slip back into the pre-Keynes, laissez-faire cycle of boom and bust. Governments intervene also to meet what they perceive to be the public need for new programs and services. Indeed, it is evasive to talk about government spending and the increase in the money supply as the causes of inflation; taxing, spending, and printing money are merely mechanisms that transmit demands from the public through the politicians to the economy. It is more precise to talk about medicare as the cause of inflation, or national defence, or new school buildings, or highways. These and a thousand other public services that lie behind the public-spending statistics compete with private spending for limited resources. In some cases, public services are obviously more important than private goods and services. For example, no one would suggest we should cut spending on the police or the armed forces in order to increase spending on, say, deodorants; or that we should build fewer miles of highways to free resources to manufacture more autos; or that we should cut back on hospitals to permit more advertising of tobacco and alcohol. On the other hand, we have to leave private business with enough money and manpower to produce the goods we want, to provide employment, and to generate tax revenues.

In short, the argument between public and private spenders, between government and business, is really one about priorities. If we can't afford all the goods and services businessmen and politicians would like to produce, how do we make the choice? (There is, incidentally, no escape from the problem in suggesting that the solution is to eliminate government waste. Public bureaucracies do waste money, but not on the scale of private business bureaucracies which manufacture obsolescence into their products and change fashions to create public demand.)

Businessmen claim that a free market – that is, letting the consumer choose where to spend his or her money – is the best way to allocate scarce resources. Business is subject to the discipline of the market in launching new products and services, they say, while government simply imposes its services on the taxpayers who have no choice in the matter. There are a couple of arguments against this proposition. The first is that governments are, in fact, subject to tough competition. Every day in the House of Commons and in the media their priorities and products are criticized. Every year they have to submit their program and spending estimates to public scrutiny. And at every election, if they have not satisfied their customers, the voters, they can be put out of business. Directors and managers of business corporations, however, are accountable only to shareholders, usually in a perfunctory way, and it is not at all clear that the market really exercises much control over the operations of the largest and most successful companies, as we shall now see in another view of what has gone wrong with the economy.

Big Business
John Kenneth Galbraith claims that major corporations are not subject to effective competition or to the choice of the consumer in the modern economy. In his influential book, *Economics and the Public Purpose*, and in earlier writings, he divides the business sector of the economy into two parts, the Planning System and the Market System. In the United States, he says, the Planning System comprises the 1,000 largest corporations that produce half of all goods and services, while the Market System comprises the remaining 12 million smaller businesses that produce the other half of private output. As the name implies, companies and farmers in the Market System are, by and large, subject to the discipline of the free market. The giants in the Planning System, however, must control the environment in which they do business in order to protect their huge investments of money and time in new technology and products. Galbraith writes:

> In specific terms this means that prices must, if possible, be under control; that decisive costs must also be under control or so managed that adverse movements can be offset by the controlled prices; that effort must be made to ensure that the consumer responds favourably to the product; that if the state is the customer, it will remain committed to the product or its

96

development; that other needed state action is arranged and any adverse government action prevented; that other uncertainties external to the firm are minimized and other external needs assured. In other words, the firm is required, with increasing technical products and processes, increasing capital, a lengthened gestation period (between the initial investment and the final emergence of a usable product) and an increasingly large and complex organization, to control or seek to the social environment in which it functions – or any part which impinges upon it. It must plan not only its own operations; it must also, to the extent possible, plan the behaviour of people and the state as these effect it. This is a matter not of ambition but of necessity.

The giant corporations dominate the markets in which they operate, and by controlling their own production they can regulate prices. By raising prices they can pass on to consumers the cost of contracts they negotiate with labour unions which are, in effect, partners in the planning system. They have political influence with government and the power of advertising and public relations to manipulate public demand and public opinion. Because they control the market rather than being controlled by it, they are largely immune to government policies designed to influence the economy through the market – for example, to control inflation by reducing demand and putting pressure on profits.

Galbraith's theory that it is not Big Government but Big Business which has weakened the market system has both supporters and critics. Prime Minister Trudeau remarked, in a CTV interview at the end of 1975, "I'm not as wise and as experienced as Galbraith but there's no doubt that his thinking has permeated my thought and that of a lot of other people." A. W. Johnson, formerly a senior federal civil servant and economic policy adviser and now president of the CBC, echoed Galbraith in a lecture at Massey College, Toronto, in 1974. Discussing current economic problems, he said: "Economic theory, and indeed its application, has not taken adequately into account the great growth in the power of corporations and unions, and their capacity to set and maintain prices and wages despite temporary declines in demand ... price and wage fixing in large sectors of the economy are administered decisions." On the other hand, one of Johnson's civil service colleagues, Simon Reisman, deputy finance minister until he resigned to become a consultant to business corporations, analysed and rejected Galbraith's thesis. In an address to the Institute for Policy Analysis at the University of Toronto in 1976, he said:

> Despite the existence of varying degrees of monopoly power in many sectors of our economy, and extensive state regulations in others, the modern industrial state in the Western World is in its essence market oriented and price sensitive. The overwhelming proportion of production, distribution and consumption is performed by individuals and institutions who seek to maximize their positions in a reasonably effective competitive environment. We are driven to the judgement that the Galbraith system rests on the most tenuous of empirical foundations. In its most fundamental aspects it is simply not accurate.

Public Expectations
Reisman offered yet another explanation of our economic problems. He argued that the root cause of inflation in Canada and other countries was the build-up of demand pressures over many years through monetary and fiscal expansion – that is, by excessive government spending and printing of money. The oil crisis and crop failures made the problem more serious, he said, but did not cause it. So why didn't this conventional inflation respond to conventional cures when government reduced demand? "The reasons why we are experiencing high inflation and high unemployment at the same time are two-fold," said Reisman. "First, there are unavoidable time lags between the adoption of economic policies and the behaviour of the economy. Second, after many years of virtually uninterrupted inflation people come to expect that it will continue and behave as if it will." In other words, don't be impatient; it takes a year or two for restraint to work. And second, the very fact that people have got used to inflation makes it harder to stop. For example, when prices have been rising at 3 per cent a year for several years, the wise businessman builds that expectation into his plans for next year, adding 3 per cent to prices, and the shrewd trade union negotiator adds 3 per cent to his wage demand, again pushing up prices.

98

Reisman's diagnosis was very similar to that offered by the Prices and Incomes Commission in 1972:

> In our view these response lags and the persistence of beliefs and patterns of behaviour formed on the basis of experience during the prolonged inflationary expansion of the 1960s are almost certainly the dominant factors in explaining recent wage and price trends. . . . Although the evidence is not sufficiently clear-cut to support dogmatic conclusions, it seems to us that such changes as appear to have occurred in the degree of monopoly power exercised by organized labor or business have not been a dominant factor in the substantial increase in costs and prices experienced over the period as a whole since the early 1960s.

In tacitly rejecting Galbraith's theory that planning has replaced the market, the commission did, however, mention an idea that underlies another theory.

Social Demands
The commission suggested that although corporations and unions may not have the power to manipulate the market directly, they do perhaps have the power to influence governments which can manipulate markets. But we can go further and say it is not only corporations and unions that make demands upon government, but the entire community that expects the government to manage the market so as to ensure full employment, non-stop growth, and social security. This idea has been well expressed by Albert T. Sommers, senior vice-president and chief economist of the Conference Board, a u.s. business group, in an article in the *Financial Analysts Journal* in 1975:

> The most general and most important cause of escalating long-term inflation in Western nations is their historical development into mixed economies. The free markets and macro-economic behaviour described by conventional economics are now, more than ever, awesome abstractions from the real world they propose to describe; they grow more remote daily, with the growth and spread of a public sector dedicated to the fulfillment of new economic and social objectives carrying ethical rather than free market warrants. . . . While mixed eco-

nomies all over the world have cheerfully validated the new goals, they have only reluctantly and only partially adapted their conventional policy equipment, inherited from an era of lesser social commitment. . . . The fallout from this collision of social progressivism with economic conservatism is inflation.

In short, the market allocates resources according to strictly economic values while modern society demands that other goals should be taken into account. We demand not merely economic efficiency, but social security for those not strong enough to compete in the market and restraints upon the super-strong who do too well in the market, together with preservation of the environment, conservation of resources, and many other goals conceived to be in the interests of the public, although not necessarily in the interests of the private businessman. When these public demands are superimposed on private demands, the market is overloaded and the result is inflation.

York University president MacDonald, in a speech in 1976, also attributed inflation to political and social changes. He conceded that Reisman had been technically correct to blame monetary and fiscal expansion by government, but added: "However, that does not change the fact that the expansion has come in response to a desire on the part of people for a higher level of government services and public goods. . . . We will continue to have a chronically high rate of inflation unless we find ways to reduce individual aspirations or ways to increase economic growth."

Equality and Inflation
In his book, *The New Inflation - The Politics of Prices and Incomes*, published in Britain in 1973, Aubrey Jones approached the subject with unusual experience and authority. Formerly an economic journalist and business executive, he became a Conservative MP and minister and was then chosen by a Labour government to become chairman to the National Board for Prices and Incomes from 1965 to 1970. He was later able to use the economic research facilities at Cambridge University to write his study of modern inflation. He traced the tendency of wages to rise faster than output, thus forcing up prices, to changes in social

100

and political attitudes which were superseding market forces. Jones argued that, in modern, democratic society, each worker feels entitled to the same pay increase as those enjoyed by the wage leaders in the most productive industries, or in those led by aggressive unions, or even in those such as airlines in which standards are international. "The franchise is now universal," reasoned Jones. "This means that, at the very least, political rights are far more equal than they ever were previously; it would be surprising, then, if 'everyman' did not attempt to extend into the economic field the political equality to which he has become accustomed." In other words, the modern worker seeks equality of pay as a right regardless of whether he or she is actually earning the pay in the market place. "If workers try to claim an increasing share of the national income, so also will shareholders," said Jones, and companies pass along these increased costs in high prices charged to consumers.

Jones went on to offer the provocative suggestion that in sophisticated political societies, the attempt by government to reduce demand pressures by creating unemployment in the conventional way may actually be counter-productive. When unemployment began to rise in Britain, he said, the reaction of trade union leaders was to demand higher wages in the hope of stimulating demand and creating more jobs. "Trade unions, which we have described as essentially political in nature, have learnt enough to be able to launch a counter-attack on an attempt by government to induce higher unemployment," he said.

While Jones' theories grew out of British experience, he also studied events in Canada, the United States, and Europe, and suggested his ideas would apply in all industrial democracies. One can certainly note in Canada events that seem to support his conclusion. It is widely accepted that when Seaway workers won a large wage settlement approved by the federal government in the mid-1960s, they set a pattern for increases across the economy, without regard for what the market could justify. Canadian workers in some industries have also tended to follow the leadership of U.S. workers, undeterred by differences in the economic conditions in the two countries. Unemployment has not discouraged high wage claims, and when the government tried to restrain incomes by imposing controls, the Canadian Labour Congress reacted by ordering a general strike.

Growth and Inflation
André Raynauld, the chairman of the Economic Council of Canada, touched on the same subject in 1975 when he blamed the state of mind created by growth and prosperity for inflation.

For a quarter of a century, growth fever has pervaded the world. Expansion opens to the mind a captivating perspective – that of a game where everybody can win, which in turn becomes the game where everybody *must* win, and the gains must be realized more and more and faster and faster. Affluence becomes something as natural as the air we breathe. Increasingly, people want everything at the same time, which is like wanting to reap the fruits of growth without accepting its imperatives. Moreover, the new private or collective preferences, such as environmental conservation, shorter work periods, management participation, and social security, both multiply needs and reduce potential supply so that they become inflation factors. As this growth develops in our "global village," the images of which are carried to hundreds of millions of people at the same time, aspirations move up and the affluence of the one creates a situation of subjective shortage for the others. Thus the improvement in the standard of living becomes a cause of increasing frustration, and a source of tension between social groups. It is no longer surprising, then, that in this rush for more the price-regulating mechanisms have stopped working. Formerly, a fiscal plan for readjustment, accompanied by the appropriate psychological conditioning, resulted in a genuine lowering of purchasing power and a slowdown of inflationary pressures. Today, increased fiscal pressure has itself become inflationary. The collective strength of producers and wage earners is more powerful than the adjustment mechanisms that are rejected by all: Higher taxes call for correspondingly higher wages.

A Conclusion
Let us now summarize this account of events and the evidence of the experts.

First, Keynes and his followers persuaded governments that they could and should intervene to correct the deficiencies and cruelties of the market system. But the governments' managers lacked the precision tools and political skills to make the system work perfectly.

The economic managers misjudged circumstances, encountered international forces outside their control, and were subject to domestic political pressures. They could not therefore prevent periods of unemployment, slow growth, and creeping inflation.

As memories of the much worse conditions of the 1930s faded, even these relatively minor failures of management became unacceptable. By the 1960s, politicians were promising, and the public was expecting, permanent full employment, expanding social services, and constantly increasing private affluence. The attempt to meet these growing expectations by fiscal and monetary stimulation of the economy created the pressures that led to the great inflation of the 1970s.

Rising prices in the postwar years had conditioned the public and meant there was less resistance than might have been expected to inflation when it began to accelerate. People simply built the expectation of higher prices into their plans, which became self-fulfilling prophecies.

The rise in profits and world oil prices, crop failures, and other international events confused the situation and made it easy to find scapegoats for inflation, but they were not the primary cause which was, as noted, excessive government stimulation in Canada and other countries.

In stimulating economies, however, governments were not acting on mere whim. They were responding to real public demands expressed through the political process and encouraged by the mass media. The public demanded not only private growth, but a vast array of public services.

The people also rejected the traditional discipline of the market. They saw no reason to accept unemployment or recession. They demanded social insurance not only against accident and ill health, but also against the judgement of the market – that is, they wanted unemployment pay for those for whom the market provided no work, welfare pay or a guaranteed income for those who could not compete, education and training for those without marketable skills, pensions for those who had not provided for their old age.

Individuals no longer accepted the economic inequality and consequent social inferiority implied by the market system. No matter what their circumstances or the economic value of their work, they began to think themselves as good as the next person and entitled to the same rewards in a democratic society.

The growth of corporations made it possible for the leaders in some industries to escape, at least in part, competition in the market. In turn, this made them amenable to demands from labour unions because they were able to pass on costs in higher prices. The unions, enjoying a new respectability in the postwar years, provided protection for their members against market forces, and set wage standards for workers not in unions.

In short, because government has been able to solve some economic problems, there is now a widespread expectation that it can solve all problems. Because we are better educated, enjoy greater social security, and have less fear of the future, we are more ambitious. We are also more democratic in the sense that we are less ready to accept that there is a natural order in which some are rich and most poor; in which some types of work are much better paid than others equally onerous; that fine homes, luxury cars, foreign vacations, lavish entertainment, and expensive restaurants are properly reserved for a social elite. We all demand, "Me too." When government fails to deliver the good life to all, we say it must be incompetent, or that it is bound to the interests of the rich and therefore an oppressor of the poor. When it imposes income and profit controls, they are accepted at best with grumbling reluctance as a temporary necessary evil.

Having rejected the discipline of the market, we are loath to accept the alternative discipline of decision by government.

NEW PROBLEMS

The problems of economic management are likely to be compounded in future by international trends outside our control. Third World countries are demanding a new economic order that would override the market and impose new demands on the developed countries. While they are not likely to be able to bring about revolutionary changes, some disruption of patterns of trade and payments seems inevitable. The growth of the supra-national system described in a later chapter opens the Canadian economy to pressures from the United States, Europe, and else-where. Concern about declining world resources of raw materials may bring about spectacular price increases; at the very least, producer-countries are likely to try to follow the example of the Organization of Petroleum Exporting Countries by forming car-tels. The world monetary system has been in a state of flux and may continue to be a source of concern and instability.

At home we face social as well as economic problems. For example, we have to decide at what rate to use our declining reserves of oil and gas and other raw materials; what degree of pollution to tolerate in the interest of industrial production; what limits to impose upon the height of downtown buildings and the sprawl of suburbs. These and many other issues obviously can-not be left to the market.

TOWARD A SOLUTION

"Basically, there are only two ways in our world of making choices and allocating resources: free and voluntary transactions or exchange as part of the market economy, and collective deci-sion-making rules which are nothing else than government coer-cion," said André Raynauld, chairman of the Economic Council, in an address to the Canadian Association of the Club of Rome in 1976. He noted that the market economy has promoted extraordinary prosperity and encouraged individual liberty, but also that it creates social costs, undesirable concentration of wealth, and instability. Governments have increasingly inter-vened to correct these deficiencies so that "we have witnessed a gradual shift from the market system to government regulation as the preferred tool for decision-making." But this has brought about its own problems, so that, "There is nowadays an over-whelming amount of criticism about the way in which the state discharges the duties that have fallen to it, whether as income distribution agent, or as regulator of economic activity. . . . The task that we have to accomplish, therefore, consists of finding a new division of responsibilities, some to be subjected to the laws of the market place, and some to the laws of Parliament. We are really talking here of a new social contract, of a 'constitutional revolution.' "

The new contract or system cannot be a return to the free market, for the reasons already discussed. The market, for all its virtues as a producer of goods and services, is not acceptable in a modern democratic society.

On the other hand, economies under complete government control do not inspire confidence or encourage imitation. The communist and socialist countries appear to avoid most of the problems of unemployment and some of the problems of inflation, but they depend on the more dynamic market economies for technological leadership. The concentration of economic power in the hands of the state also makes easier the concentration of political power and denial of liberty, although this is not an inevitable development. Indeed, social reformers must believe that we can learn to manage our economic affairs by democratic decision-making, just as we manage our political affairs, and that public ownership and control of economic resources will eventually enlarge liberty. But it would be foolish to ignore the dangers inherent in state control, and best to proceed cautiously.

We are left for the moment with the so-called mixed economy in which both public authorities and the private sector play important roles. But the essence of our problem is that the mixed economy has not been working well. The addition of public spending to private demand has exceeded the capacity of the economy. It is unrealistic to believe that government can or will reduce significantly its level of spending and activity in order to return power to the market. Even under politicians who claim to be conservatives, government continues to grow in response to inescapable problems and public demand for services.

So while we may experience periods of conservatism, or slow-growth of the public sector, over the long haul we must expect to see an expanding public sector. The issue is how to reconcile public and private needs – that is, to create a mechanism more democratic, more fair, more acceptable than the market, which will enable us to choose between public and private services while keeping the total of demand in balance with supply so that we suffer neither excessive demand and inflation nor under-demand and unemployment.

106

Income and Profit Controls

Governments in Canada and other democracies have been experimenting for years with the mechanism of such an incomes policy to supplement fiscal and monetary policies. Price and income controls were accepted during the war as a necessary tool for managing the economy in the national interest, but with the peace they were happily abolished in favour of a return to the market. When it began to appear in the 1960s, however, that the market could not manage the economy in an acceptable way, Louis Rasminsky, governor of the Bank of Canada, was among the first to suggest that an incomes policy would be helpful. He pointed out that agreement to restrain the rise of incomes would reduce the need to use the blunt and painful weapons of fiscal and monetary policies. The government in 1965 asked the Economic Council to examine the idea of income and price controls, but the council, strongly influenced by trade union opinion, decided they would be useful only in an emergency. But by 1968, with inflation becoming more serious, the government appointed the Prices and Incomes Commission to recommend a solution. The commission soon moved beyond research to seek the agreement of the federal and provincial governments, business and labour to a policy of voluntary restraint. The effort failed, mainly because the Canadian Labour Congress and the Confederation of National Trade Unions refused to co-operate and the provincial governments were less than enthusiastic. The government then turned back to the conventional fiscal and monetary squeeze, but as we have seen that also proved both unsuccessful and politically unacceptable.

The Prices and Incomes Commission continued its research and in its final report in 1972 foresaw serious difficulties in trying to defeat deep-seated inflationary expectations with conventional policies: "To be successful, an attempt to rely on demand restraint alone to restore reasonable price stability in such circumstances may well require the acceptance of abnormally high unemployment over an extended period. It is in a situation of this kind that our analysis suggests a potentially useful role for a temporary program of controls." The commission argued, in effect, that with determined leadership by government and strong public support, controls on incomes and prices could help to break inflationary expectations and reinforce conventional policies.

Conservative leader Robert Stanfield adopted this proposal in 1973, proposing a ninety-day freeze on incomes and prices, to be followed by eighteen months to two years of selective controls. He speculated in conversation that in fact some more permanent system of controls might be necessary to manage the modern economy, but insisted on the platform that he would introduce only temporary controls, as a way of reducing expectations and restoring the power of the market. When he made controls the major plank in his platform in the 1974 election, the government turned it against him. Ignoring the report of his own commission, Trudeau argued effectively that inflation was being imported from abroad, in the form of higher prices for oil, food and other goods. Controls in Canada could not freeze foreign prices, he said. In this, he had the powerful support of David Lewis, leader of the NDP, who had campaigned in 1972 on the misleading proposition that corporations were ripping-off consumer and taxpayers by raising prices to reap excessive profits. Having persuaded many Canadians that profits were the villain of inflation, Lewis had to oppose restraints on wages.

Back in power, the Liberal government was again faced with the problem of inflation, and in his budget speech in November 1974, Finance Minister John Turner began to edge cautiously toward a form of controls. "The sum total of all the claims on the nation's resources – however justified they may seem to be – clearly exceeds what is in fact available to be shared," he said, identifying the root of inflation. The solution was, "To find a better way of reconciling the competing interests of the various groups which make up our society." Turner was talking about an incomes policy. With other members of the Cabinet, he began discussions with business, labour, and other groups. "We sought a consensus on a new framework to govern the setting of incomes and prices in a manner which would be fairer to all," he reported in his 1975 budget. But, "consensus on a set of voluntary guidelines has not been reached." Turner continued:

In contrast to the situation in 1973 and 1974 when our inflation primarily reflected international forces, and controls couldn't possibly have worked, we are now faced with escalating domestic costs in an under-employed economy. In these circumstances, controls could provide the most direct response to the problem. Thus, unlike our position on severe monetary and fiscal restraint, we did not reject controls in principle. Indeed, in one respect they would have had an advantage over a voluntary consensus. By using the powers of the law to make all groups obey the rules, each would have had the assurance that all would be making a contribution. But there would have been – and are – immense difficulties and disadvantages in such a course of action. Government would have had to interfere in every type of business decision and wage settlement. To a far greater extent than in a voluntary program, a new bureaucratic apparatus would have to be set up. New types of inequity would be created. The flexibility of the market economy in directing resources where they are most needed would be impaired. Dislocation would occur.

These costs would be worth paying if direct controls could be successfully imposed. If this were the case, we might well achieve lower price and cost increases without higher unemployment. But the success of such a program would depend crucially on widespread public support. As I have said before, I believe that we can resort to direct controls only when there is a public conviction of the need for such action. That point has not been reached.

The point was, however, reached a few months later when Turner unexpectedly resigned from the Cabinet to return to private life, leaving behind the raging inflation and rising unemployment he had failed to curb. There were rumours he resigned because of disagreement with Trudeau over policy, but Trudeau denied this and Turner did not dispute his word. In any event, Turner's sensational resignation created a crisis of confidence for the government, adding to the public pressure that it take firm action to demonstrate that it still had the will to control events.

The provincial premiers, at their annual conference, volunteered to support the federal government if it decided to introduce controls. The Economic Council, meeting in October, emphasized the gravity of inflationary trends and "concluded that demand management policies alone were insufficient to yield full employment and price stability in the foreseeable future and that additional new policy instruments were required." Simon Reisman, the Deputy Finance Minister and thus the senior civil service adviser on economic policy, overcame his doubts and recommended temporary controls. "I did this to help push the government off dead-centre in a near desperate situation," he disclosed later, after leaving the government.

On October 13, the government finally acted. Trudeau broadcast to the nation the news that controls were to be applied to the 1,500 largest companies and their employees, and to professional people for three years. He said the federal government would impose the guidelines on itself and its employees, and he asked the provincial governments to follow suit. Finally, he appealed to all other Canadians to accept the guidelines voluntarily.

In coming reluctantly to controls after years of hesitation, the Canadian government was following a familiar pattern. British Conservative leader Edward Heath won office promising to set the economy free by abolishing the controls instituted by the Labour government, but soon found himself forced by inflation to try again to impose guidelines. Labour bitterly opposed the Conservative program, but on return to office set about persuading the unions to accept a new "social contract" which involved severe limits on wage claims. In the United States, President Richard Nixon was declaring his faith in a free economy up to the eve of imposing controls. In each case, controls were accepted only as a necessary evil when all else had failed. They were imposed only for limited periods and, perhaps for that reason, enjoyed only very limited success. There was no incentive to reconsider fundamental attitudes and objectives when all assumed that after a brief period of controls it would be possible to return to business as usual in the market.

After Controls

When Prime Minister Trudeau cautiously questioned the comfortable assumption that no long-range changes were necessary, business and labour arose as one to denounce him. In a series of broadcasts, speeches, and interviews at the end of 1975 and the beginning of 1976, Trudeau raised the question of what was going to happen at the end of the three-year period of controls. He spoke of the need for a new society with new values, pointed out that the market or mixed economy was not working well when it produced high inflation and high unemployment, and talked about the need for more rather than less government intervention in future.

"The only benefit of having restraint imposed by law is that it gives people time to understand and adopt the real cure, which is a basic change in our attitudes – a realization that we cannot expect incomes to continue growing at a faster rate than the economy itself is growing," he said in his TV speech announcing the controls program. "For if that realization does not become deeply imbedded in our national consciousness, if we do not succeed in changing our attitudes and expectations, if Canadians in great numbers do not agree to practise voluntary self-restraint, then, as surely as night follows day, the rate of inflation will explode upward as soon as the government's restraining rules are removed."

At the Liberal party's policy convention the following month, Trudeau went a little further: "It's not the law, it's not the strength of controls which will lick inflation. . . . It's much deeper than that. We want to bring in a new set of values in Canada which will permit Canadians henceforth to develop their great society without resorting to controls."

In December, Trudeau again broadcast to the nation to announce the measures the government was taking to restrain its own spending, and he threw in a few closing remarks: "I will be speaking to you again in the coming months about the new kind of society we will need to create in response to the new economic circumstances in which we are living, here in Canada and throughout the world. I will be speaking to you about the need for new attitudes toward economic growth and exploitation of our natural resources – new attitudes toward labour-management relations, social co-operation, and the sharing of our wealth."

In a year-end interview broadcast by CTV on December 28, Bruce Phillips and Carol Taylor questioned Trudeau about what he meant by a new society and drew some rambling answers:

People are really realizing it's a different world and that you can't live in a different world with the same institutions and the same values you had before. . . . The values which served in other times, in other civilizations, were probably values which could serve well now. Belief in sharing, belief in being good trustees of what we have, tolerance, belief in freedom and ordinance. I don't think that when you get to the philosophical level you call for a different type of human being. I do think that the habits that we've acquired and the behaviours we've acquired in two or three hundred years of industrial society have led to sending the system out of joint. . . . We haven't been sharing much and we haven't been living in a brotherly-love way and that is part of the problem. . . .

There is new thinking and there are new institutions developing. Many people, I think, still see those controls as . . . a bit of strong medicine we'll have to take in order to get inflation down, but it's really more than that. . . . It's a massive intervention into the decision-making power of the economic groups and it's telling Canadians we haven't been able to make it work, the free market system. We've ended up with very high unemployment and very high inflation. We can't go back to what was before with the same habits, the same behaviour and the same institutions, otherwise we'd be back to high unemployment and high inflation. I've seen . . . some economists say all you've got to do is get back to the free market system and make this market system work. It won't, you know. We can't destroy the big unions and we can't destroy the multinationals. We can control them, but who will control them? The government. That means the government is going to take a larger role in running institutions, as we're doing now with our anti-inflation controls, but as we'll be presumably doing even after the controls are ended because, I repeat, we don't want to go back to the same kind of society with unemployment and high inflation, and this means you're going to have also big governments and it's not simply a matter of saying this government is spending too much and if they'd only cut down things would go better. Things don't necessarily get better because we spend less on health or on welfare and leave the private sector free to spend more on producing bobbles or multicoloured gadgets. The state is important. The government is important. It means there is going to be not less authority in our lives but perhaps more. . . .

I view this control period as a breathing space. Give us time to make the changes and I think that at the end of the three years we will be able to decontrol a great deal of sectors and a great deal of people, but I say frankly . . . it's probably likely that at the end of three years we will have to retain control on those who either haven't played ball or on those who haven't demonstrated that given a decontrolled economy, we will have acquired the new virtues of self-discipline and self-restraint and living within our means.

The reaction to the Prime Minister's philosophizing was so fierce that he had to arrange to make a speech to the Canadian Club in Ottawa on January 19 to answer his critics.

While accepting the need to intervene, he explained, the Liberal government rejected socialism, corporatism, and statism and had no desire to interfere in those sections of the economy "where free enterprise is strong, where individual initiative, independence and risk-taking are present, where self-reliant men and women continue to build a better life for themselves and their communities by investing their time, their capital and their abilities in ways which add to the strength of Canada and its people." But he argued:

Some extreme free enterprisers have suggested that our best hope for the future lies in the creation of a true free market economy, a market system designed according to economists' models of perfect competition. I believe they are wrong. Such a system would involve, for example, the breaking up of some of our giant corporations and unions. Do we really want to do that, even if we could? Before you say, "Yes," ask yourself how Canada could be largely self-sufficient in steel, for example, if we didn't have some very large steel companies capable of amassing the enormous amount of capital needed for the job, the sophisticated technology, the managerial experience and skilled labour force. We need some large corporations, because of their efficiency, because of their unique ability to do the jobs that need to be done, because of their ability to sustain and increase our export trade.

113

The problem is not the existence of monopolies or quasi-monopolies in certain sectors of our economy. The problem is how to ensure that their power is used in the public interest, and is directed toward the achievement of national goals.

In that context, the issue before us is to what extent we will be controlled by government regulation, and to what extent we will be controlled by our own sense of responsibility. I think we all favour as little of the former and as much of the latter as is humanly possible.

Trudeau pointed out that if the private sector wanted to avoid government solutions to the problems he had mentioned, business and labour would have to provide their own answers. How would they prevent strikes, clean up pollution, distribute economic development more equitably across Canada, conserve energy, relate wages to productivity, waste less food?

While Trudeau recognized the basic changes underlying economic pressures and made clear there could be no return to business as usual, he was confusing in his prescription. He accepted at least part of Galbraith's theory of a Planning System outside the control of the market, but rejected Galbraith's solution of permanent price and income controls. He argued the inevitability of Bigger Government, but then invited Big Business and Big Labour to show how they could get along without government policing. Time and again he returned to the idealistic notion that the solution to economic problems lay in a change of human values; a return, he said at one point, to the values of pre-industrial society.

Labour and the Left

Although examination of the Prime Minister's texts suggests that he was confused and confusing and unrealistic about human nature, there were many critics who were quite sure that behind his rhetoric lay a plot to abolish free enterprise and impose a tyranny. Businessmen were bitterly critical of Trudeau for his remarks about the failure of the market system, but probably the most outspoken opponent was Joe Morris, president of the Canadian Labour Congress, who declared: "There is no further need for speculation about the government's true purpose. The stated policy of the federal government is to centralize political power in Ottawa. The vehicle by which this will be effectively accomplished is the anti-inflation control program." Morris appeared to have in mind the idea that Trudeau was imposing some form of corporate state descended from fascism and Nazism – a thesis aired earlier by Wayne Chevaldayoff, *The Globe and Mail's* economic affairs reporter in Ottawa.

It was revealing but not surprising that the CLC took the lead in defending the market system against government regulation. Although associated with the NDP in Canada and with left-wing parties in Europe, labour unions are one of the main bulwarks of the capitalist system. Their reason for existence is to bargain with capital to improve the conditions of labour, and they have done well in this market system. Paul Johnson, a British socialist writing in the left-wing weekly, *The New Statesman,* in 1975, accused:

> The trade union is a product of nineteenth century capitalism. It is part of that system. Against powerful, highly organized and ruthless capitalist forces, it had an essential, even noble part to play. But when those forces are disarmed; when they are in headlong retreat – indeed howling for mercy – the union has no function to perform. . . . Yet it is still carrying on doing the only thing it knows how to do – ask for higher wages. As it has beaten all its opponents, as it is for all practical purposes the state, it naturally gets them. A subject government prints the money, and the result is inflation on an unprecedented scale. British trade unionism has thus become a formula for national misery.

Canadian trade unions have only a fraction of the power of their British counterparts, and Canadian capitalists are hardly howling for mercy. But it is true that Canadian unions have considerable power at the bargaining table, as well as a fair amount of influence in politics through their affiliation with the NDP and their access to ministers, the media to promote their views, and their role in advisory bodies, such as the Economic Council. They have often put their influence to good use in pressing for social reform, but they are not responsible to anyone except their members for the demands they make on the economy through their wage claims. Just as businessmen charge the highest price the trade will bear to make the maximum profit, trade unionists extract as much as they can in wages and benefits, by negotiation and by strike action. In the Planning System where the employer can pass the cost along to the customers, the unionists are in practice obtaining their higher standard by forcing down the standard of someone less powerful in the community.

Income controls severely limit union power; therefore, said Raynauld in his speech to the Club of Rome Association: "Organized labour now appears to be the staunchest supporter of the market economy." Morris made clear in speeches and statements that the CLC was opposing not merely the level of incomes and prices established by the controls, which it claimed were unfair, but also the very concept of controls, which it saw as a threat to democracy. The CLC withdrew from the Economic Council and other bodies to show its unwillingness to co-operate with government. But this was an uncomfortable and in the long run untenable position for the union movement.

The NDP, like all social democratic and socialist parties, had always criticized the market system and proposed instead state planning, which would obviously involve some form of incomes policy. But although the NDP leaders loyally supported the CLC in its attack on the Trudeau government, they could hardly approve the attack on the very principle of controls and the defence of the market system. The NDP Premier of Manitoba, Ed Schreyer, in an interview with *Maclean's* magazine in March 1976, disclosed that one of the reasons he refused an invitation to seek the leadership of the federal party was his disagreement with labour. He argued that controls were vital in the new economy, but he found that unions were "fundamentally opposed to restraints in the marketplace, and they'll continue to react against them as unnecessary and undesirable. . . . Oh, it'll change eventually, but I'm afraid of the kind of political agony we'll have to endure before that." Another of the party's intellectual leaders, Charles Taylor, in a Massey College lecture on "The Politics of the Steady State," looked beyond economic growth and foresaw the need for a comprehensive system of rationing, subsidies, and other controls to establish a minimum standard for all, as the alternative to dictatorship. Galbraith, who is sometimes described as a socialist and is certainly the most fashionable of the new economists, continued to advocate controls in books and articles and interviews. In *The New Statesman,* in February 1976, he declared:

The first practical step toward stability without unemployment must be to control income claims. There is no alternative. This, however, cannot be done for trade unions while leaving upper-middle-class income and that of the rich untouched, elegant as may be the argument for so doing. From this circumstance comes the basic macroeconomic policy to which the democratic Left in all countries must adhere. . . . The trade unions must be persuaded to hold their claims to what can be afforded out of increased productivity gains. And then, as a matter of essential equity, the consumption claims of upper income groups must be subject to effective restraint, increasing in stringency as income increases so that the aggregate of claims does not exceed the capacity to produce. Where there is substantial corporate market power, this requires control of prices and therewith of profits.

When Robert Lewis of *Maclean's* magazine interviewed Galbraith in 1976, and pointed out that labour in Canada was opposed to controls, Galbraith replied:

The acceptance comes from the discovery that the alternatives are worse. We see this process most clearly in Britain where one has a trade union movement of high intelligence, great honesty, great stubbornness of thought – but which has now come to accept that a comprehensive system of wage controls is better than heavy unemployment or inflation. The AFL-CIO in the United States accept the policy on incomes. The Swedish trade unions, the Benelux trade unions, the German trade unions have been bargaining within this context for years. They have been recognizing that if they go beyond a certain point they limit exports and that the repercussions hurt their own members. The step the British and Canadian governments have taken, which the Democratic candidates are coming around to, is a big one; a major modification of collective bargaining as it has always been known; the abandonment of private price-making by large corporations as it has always been known; a public policy towards other incomes. This is the largest step in economic policy since the Keynesian revolution,

117

perhaps larger even than that. This was a step that had to come gradually, that had to wait for the kind of consensus that the alternatives – unemployment and inflation – were worse.

At the CLC convention in May 1976, President Morris and other leaders escalated their rhetorical attack on controls and received permission from the rank and file to call a general strike. But they also agreed to discuss with the government planning for the future of the economy. The CLC's paradoxical position seemed to be that once it had demonstrated its strength by forcing the government to withdraw controls, it would then sit down as an equal with government and business to plan controls. The paradox was not, however, important. The significant fact was that the CLC was coming to accept the concept of a planned rather than a market economy. Soon after the convention, Morris and others began exploratory meetings with Trudeau and his ministers.

Business and Controls
Business was less alarmed by controls than the CLC. As Raynauld said: "Business, on the whole, being already quite familiar with a close government presence, reacted coolly to this development." Business, in fact, had always been willing to co-operate in the several proposals for voluntary guidelines on prices and incomes. But business leaders were very upset when Trudeau began to talk about a new society in which some form of controls would be permanent, and were not reassured by his statement that the government would preserve and encourage private enterprise wherever possible. They remained deeply suspicious of the Prime Minister's intentions. But major corporations have always recognized that it is in their best interest to work closely with government, and there is no reason to suppose there would be immovable business opposition to a form of public planning and control.

Economic Planning
Public planning is now clearly developing in the new economy, and the remaining question is what form it will take. Raynauld has suggested that government, business, labour, and perhaps other representative bodies should engage in a planning exercise

118

to set goals and targets for the future, in order to re-establish social consensus. As political decision-making is tending to increase in scope as compared with the market system, he said, public participation in economic planning is "indispensable if we wish to preserve a live and effective democracy in which the will of the people to be governed is obvious and unconstrained."

The Senate Special Committee on Science Policy, in its report on "Targets and Strategies for the Seventies," urged that each major manufacturing industry should set up a joint management-labour task force, under a chairman appointed by government, to plan for the future, and submit proposals to a special Cabinet committee.

William A. Dimma, then Dean of Administrative studies at York University, said at a conference on business and government affairs that it was unrealistic to think of slashing government activities to restore the historical relationship with business, and undesirable to drift toward a form of socialism. He urged the need "to bring private and public sectors together in a co-operative mode. A new inter-sector contract needs to be drawn that provides benefits to all parties."

Beland H. Honderich, publisher of the Toronto *Star,* Canada's largest paper, said at the company's annual meeting in 1976:

> What I would suggest is that the Prime Minister, the Government and Parliament itself take the lead in establishing a series of national conferences to identify our major problems and develop possible solutions. A series of conferences to establish national goals and how to reach them should have no political, social, economic or cultural boundaries. They should be an innovative, grass-roots, apolitical if you will, search for a blueprint to shape the country's future. They should go beyond the traditional involvement of big business, big labour and their associations and power groups. They should invite, specifically, the small businessman, pensioners, farmers, non-union workers and the unorganized people in society."

In a study for the federal labour department, Charles Connaghan, an expert on industrial relations, proposed: "By bringing together for periodic review of the economy such groups as the banks, financial institutions, business organizations, trade unions and all levels of government, it would be the intention to influence these groups to realistically evaluate the true state of the economy before placing undue pressure on it by the imposition of higher interest rates, increased prices or high wage demands." Deputy Labour Minister T.M. Eberlee, reporting this idea in a speech at Queen's University in May, 1976, commented: "To me, Mr. Connaghan's proposition makes a great deal of sense."

What these and many other similar proposals reveal is a lack of confidence in the ability of existing political institutions to manage our affairs and plan for the future. Some of the reasons for lack of confidence were examined earlier – the unrepresentative nature of Parliament, the inefficiency of its operations, the confusion over constitutional responsibilities, and the competition between federal and provincial governments. One way of centralizing federal and provincial economic powers and responsibilities has been suggested on pages 60-62. But, as Aubrey Jones pointed out in *The New Inflation,* the basic problem may be that the real interest groups in modern society are not directly represented in Parliament. Parliament originally was made up of the Estates that held power in medieval society: the nobles and landowners, the clergy, and later the merchants. The new Estates are labour and capital, but their leaders do not sit in Parliament. The political parties may have a preference for labour or for capital, but in order to win election, they have to seek to represent all interests. We have forgotten, said Jones, Benjamin Disraeli's dictum that, "The great art in creating an efficient Representative Government is to secure its representation of those interests of the country which are at the same time not only considerable, but in their nature permanent." Jones argued the need for new institutions through which government could meet with business and labour and perhaps other interests to translate the general policy of Parliament into rules for prices and incomes.

We should adapt this idea to Canadian circumstances, if only for the purposes of public education and persuasion in the preparation of the annual budget. The government should convene every year, or more often if circumstances require, an open conference of groups with important interests in the state of the economy – provincial governments, business, labour, agriculture, the professions, the social welfare organizations. With advice from the public and private economic forecasting organizations, they could discuss the outlook and the claims which each proposes to make. The government could explain its policy options and seek reaction. It would be wrong to expect consensus to emerge from so many conflicting interests, but those involved in the discussions would have a better idea of realistic options and trade-offs between one goal and another. The public should be encouraged to watch live TV coverage of the conference, and every assistance should be given to schools, universities, and private organizations wishing to organize discussion groups.

The conference would not have the power to impose decisions; that would remain to the elected representatives of the people in Parliament. But laws governing prices and incomes might be less necessary, or at least better understood and accepted, after a conference to explore alternatives. Competing private interest groups would certainly find it more difficult to justify to the public an unreasonable claim for income or profit or social security benefit, and government would find it hard to explain excessive spending. In time, Parliament and the provinces might wish to give formal constitutional recognition to such a forum of interest groups and delegate to it the administration of price and income policy.

In summary, analysis of the experience of the past ten years shows beyond doubt that all industrial democracies are moving away from the market economy toward public planning and control. It is not a matter of ideology, but of necessity, widely recognized even by those who would prefer to retain as much of the market system as possible for reasons both of economic efficiency and political liberalism. The question is whether we wait for economic crisis or even disaster to drive us into state planning and control, which might turn out to be authoritarian, or whether we advance by agreement among reasonable people toward a more rational way of organizing our economic affairs. An enormous opportunity awaits the political leader with courage and capacity to begin the business of democratizing the process by which economic decisions are made.

6

Poverty

The Economic Council reported in 1968: "Poverty in Canada is real. Its numbers are not in the thousands but in the millions. There is more of it than our society can tolerate, more than our economy can afford, and far more than existing measures can cope with." Billions of dollars have since been poured into programs that were supposed to relieve poverty, but the problem has become worse rather than better. As one wit remarked; "We declared war on poverty, but poverty won." In the new society we shall have to make another attempt to conquer poverty by bringing about a more equitable distribution of the national income. It will not be easy, as the disappointing experience of the past nine years shows. The problem is not well understood, and the solution is far from clear. But it is essential for the health of our democracy to narrow the gap between the poor and the middle and upper income classes. As Statistics Canada pointed out in *Perspective Canada*, a compendium of statistics measuring the state of society published in 1974, "Income and wealth give individuals command over goods and services, and convey social and economic status." In other words, the rich enjoy not only the lion's share of the output of the economy, but also the prestige to influence events. The poor are third- or fourth-class citizens, the victims of events beyond their control. "Power is at the heart of the question," explained Andrew Hacker in *The New York Review of Books*, in May 1975, in an article about the distribution of wealth in the United States. "Some people have more freedom, more independence than others. Some are buffeted from birth to death, never in a position to bend events or answer back to authority." Gross inequalities of income and wealth are therefore incompatible in the long run with democracy, which seeks to ensure at least a reasonable equality of power among its citizens. It is for this reason that we must reject the complacent view that once we have raised all citizens above the level of subsistence, we can concentrate on encouraging the most productive persons by offering lavish rewards. In a democracy, the drive for equality is not an optional extra; it is the engine of the system.

The criticism commonly raised is that while equality is fine in theory, in practice any attempt to transfer money from the "successful" to the "unsuccessful" tends to weaken the incentive to work and, if carried too far, will eventually reduce everyone to a state of poverty. The argument is valid to a point. We are not ready for the ideal society in which each will voluntarily contribute to the maximum of ability and consume only according to need. Since we must have, therefore, some way to encourage effort and penalize sloth, there is bound to be an income gap. But there is no reason to believe that if we now try a little harder to narrow the gap – not to close it entirely – economic disaster will follow. Despite the past warnings of the rich, taxes and social service have not yet destroyed incentive. In fact, our economy is more productive than ever. After all, even in a free market the cold laws of economics do not reign supreme. Considerations of family, friendship, and simple charity influence private decisions and the allocation of resources. The welfare state seeks merely to institutionalize these decent human emotions, substituting to some extent a public judgement about how much economic efficiency to sacrifice in the cause of social justice.

There is also the argument that the real choice is not between equality and inequality, but between equality and freedom. It is said that only by severely limiting freedom of choice and enterprise can the state impose equality upon people born with unequal abilities. But freedom means something different to different income groups. For the rich, it means freedom from undue interference by the state in their private affairs; for the poor, it means freedom from hunger, sickness, and unremitting toil. If the two freedoms are indeed in conflict, the rich can better afford to give a little ground.

In seeking greater equality, however, the object is not to despoil the rich for the benefit of the poor. In a society in which the majority are not poor and have some hope of getting rich, policies aimed at radical redistribution of income would have little support. The proposal is merely to continue and make more effective the existing policy of social justice – that is, the system of progressive taxation and income guarantees. The rich would be required to pay a fairer share of taxes and perhaps to surrender some of their capital, but they would remain relatively wealthy. In an expanding economy, the middle-income groups would have to forgo some part of the rising flow of income to allow the poor to narrow the gap. In a zero-growth economy, redistribution would be more difficult, but even more necessary to achieve social stability. Fair shares would have to replace growth and rising affluence as the central principle around which to organize the society.

Before we examine the existence of poverty in Canada, let us be clear what is meant by the term in modern society. There are few Canadians who suffer from absolute poverty in the sense that they lack food, shelter, and the other bare necessities of life. Those who do live in want and perhaps die of hardship are social misfits, unable for one reason or another to make use of the public and private services which would gladly raise them above subsistence level. This is not to criticize the misfits, but to make the point that if solutions to their problems exist they are social and medical rather than financial or economic. For example, redistribution of income will not relieve the shameful conditions of native people living in poverty and despair because they cannot relate to the industrial society. The type of poverty we are discussing here is not absolute poverty, but relative poverty – that is, lack of sufficient income to share the style and standard of life of the majority of people in society, and the consequent feelings of inferiority.

J. K. Galbraith, with his flair for a descriptive phrase, defined the problem of the relatively poor in this way: "They cannot have what the larger community regards as the minimum necessary for decency; and they cannot wholly escape, therefore, the judgement of the larger community that they are indecent." A U.S. study said the definition of poverty should include "social and political exclusion," and in Canada, the Economic Council declared: "To feel poverty is, among other things, to feel oneself an unwilling outsider – a virtual non-participant in the society in which one lives." The Special Senate Committee on Poverty said in its 1971 report: "Poverty is always relative to a given time and place. The differences between Canadian and Asian poverty do not make the former any more tolerable. The poor in Canada are judged, and judge themselves, relative to the general situation in their own country, at any given point in time." Three researchers who resigned from the staff of the Senate Committee when they thought it was shirking the issues published a book titled *The Real Poverty Report* in which they said: "To be poor in our society is to suffer the most outrageous kinds of violence perpetrated by human beings on other human beings. From the very beginning, when you are still a child, you must learn to undervalue yourself. You are told you are poor because your father is too stupid or too shiftless to find a decent job. Or that he is a good for nothing who has abandoned you to a mother who cannot cope. And as you grow up on the streets, you are told your mother is dirty and lazy and that is why she has to take money from the welfare department."

In modern society, a television set is regarded as a necessity by most families and is sometimes used as a symbol to illustrate the concept of relative poverty. If one family has a black and white TV set, the neighbouring family that has only a radio feels deprived until it manages to acquire a TV. But then the first family moves up to colour TV, and the second family is again dissatisfied and poor. One can raise interesting questions about a society that measures affluence and poverty in terms of TV sets, but the fact is we don't have tools for measuring the quality of life, as distinct from the quantity of possessions. In measuring the extent of poverty, we have to measure dollar incomes. While this criterion leaves out such factors as health and environment and blurs the distinction between rural and urban lifestyles, the fact remains that it is shortage of money that keeps most of the poor feeling poor – feeling inferior and alienated and unable to play a more active role in society.

THE EXTENT OF POVERTY

The Economic Council said: "The statement that at least one Canadian in every five suffers from poverty does not appear to be a wild exaggeration." The Senate committee put it higher: one Canadian in four. The National Council of Welfare, which conducts research and advises the federal Minister of National Health and Welfare, reported that in 1970 24.5 per cent of all children under sixteen were living in poverty – a total of about 1,600,000 kids.

Such estimates are calculated by reference to what is called a "poverty line" – that is, the level of income below which a family should be considered to be poor in our affluent society. Several attempts have been made to establish poverty lines, and the differences between them account for the different estimates of how many Canadians are poor.

Statistics Canada surveyed a sample of 2,000 families and calculated that in 1961 they spent on the average about half their incomes on such basic essentials as food, clothing, and shelter. They could use the other half more or less as they saw fit to meet less basic requirements and to develop their own potentials. This estimate led to the conclusion that families spending more than 70 per cent of income on basics should be considered to be poor. The Economic Council adopted this definition for its own study, and it is still widely used, although the figures are updated from year to year to take account of the rise in the cost of living. By this 1961 measure, we have been doing quite well in reducing the proportion of families living below the poverty line. The figure has dropped, for example, from 18.4 per cent in 1967 to 15.9 per cent in 1971 to 11.4 per cent in 1973 and 9.8 per cent in 1974.

But while the poor have been raising their incomes faster than the cost of living, the middle and upper income groups have been improving their position even faster. Instead of spending half their incomes on necessities, they now spend only about 40 per cent. In 1969 StatsCan decided that this general rise in the level of affluence ought to be taken into account in setting the poverty line. When the whole society grows richer, the relative poverty line has to move up. So families who spend 62 per cent or more on essentials are now "in straitened circumstances." The Canadian Council on Social Development bases its poverty line on 50 per cent of average family income, so the line moves up with the general level of income in the country. The Senate committee on poverty, which began its study in 1968, rejected the original StatsCan formula precisely because it did not take into account rising community standards – that is, relativity. The senators worked out their own formula based on average family income, taking into account such factors as the amount of income tax paid. After several years experience, it appears that the Senate formula produces a poverty line that is always about 56 per cent of average income. This percentage is the most generous poverty line in use in Canada, which is an interesting commentary on the idea that senators are always reactionary old men.

According to these relative measurements, we haven't been reducing poverty by much, if at all. The Canadian Council on Social Development reported 18.1 per cent of families were below its poverty line in 1967 and 18.2 per cent in 1973. By the Senate standard, 23.3 per cent were poor in 1967 and 22.2 per cent in 1973. Under the revised StatsCan formula, the figure dropped from 13.4 per cent in 1973 to 11.3 per cent in 1974.

Another way of looking at what has happened to the distribution of income is to divide the population into five groups of 20 per cent each according to the level of income, and then to see what share of the total each received. According to StatsCan, the share of total income going to the poorest 20 per cent of Canadians (families and unattached individuals) actually declined from 4.4 per cent in 1965 to 4 per cent in 1974. The share going to the richest 20 per cent rose from 41.4 per cent to 42.5 per cent. To group the figures in a different way, the share going to the poorest 40 per cent dropped from 16.2 per cent to 14.9 per cent, and the share going to the richest 40 per cent rose from 65.9 per cent to 67.4 per cent. The middle 20 per cent received about the same share.

We have to remind ourselves that the total of income was rising so that while the share of the poor declined in percentage terms it rose in dollar terms. The upper limit of income received by the lowest 20 per cent rose from $2,403 in 1965 to $4,627 in 1974 – a substantial jump which, as we have seen, raised many families above the earlier poverty line. But in the same period, the income limits for the higher groups rose even faster, to $8,927 for the second 20 per cent, $13,060 for the third group, $18,238 for the fourth group. And for the richest, the sky was the limit. These figures show that in dollar terms the gap between rich and poor widened swiftly. In 1965, the best-off in the fifth, or bottom, 20 per cent were about $6,000 behind the best-off in the fourth group; by 1974 the gap had opened to more than $13,600.

StatsCan does not survey the distribution of wealth – in the form of assets such as cash in the bank, stocks and bonds, house and cottage, car and so on – as often as income. But a 1970 study showed the most wealthy one per cent of Canadians held 12 per cent of all the assets. The most wealthy 10 per cent held more than 40 per cent. The richest half of the population owned more than 90 per cent of the assets – leaving little for the poorer half. However, if the middle and upper income groups own the largest homes, the biggest cars, and the fattest bank accounts, they also tend to have larger debts, so that the gap between the net worth of the rich and the poor is perhaps not quite as dramatic as the figures on assets suggest.

Nevertheless, NDP leader Ed Broadbent claimed in a 1976 speech:

> Wealth remains grotesquely distributed. Today the bottom half of the population owns only about 2 per cent of all the stocks, bonds and mortgages. In contrast, the top 10 per cent owns about 70 per cent of the total. Eighty per cent of Canadian families do not own any Canada Savings Bonds. Four per cent of families own 65 per cent. Two per cent of Canadian families hold 67 per cent of all pension interests. And less than one per cent hold 64 per cent of the total mortgage investments.

We have to be careful in interpreting all these figures. An income below the poverty line does not necessarily mean that the recipient is suffering hardship and feels alienated from affluent society. Students, for example, often have low incomes, but high expectations for the future. Old people who own their own home and are content to live quietly, with no aspiration to move up in society, can get by happily on far less than an ambitious young family. There are some obvious problems also in comparing the cash incomes of rural and city families. Rural people may live off the land to some extent and enjoy a quality of environment not available to the slum-dweller. But these reservations should not blind us to the fact that there is a great deal of real and painful deprivation. As the National Council of Welfare put it:

> To be born poor is to face a greater likelihood of ill-health – in infancy, in childhood and throughout your adult life. To be born poor is to face a lesser likelihood that you will finish high school; still lesser that you will attend university. To be born poor is to face a greater likelihood that you will be judged a delinquent in adolescence and, if so, a greater likelihood that you will be sent to a correctional institution. To be born poor is to have the deck stacked against you at birth, to find life an uphill struggle ever after.

In a study of class cleavages published in *Political Parties in Canada,* N.H. Chi declared: "Except for the Korean War years, the gap between the rich and poor increased dramatically at a geometric rate. Rising inequality was accompanied by increases in various social malaises." He suggested a relationship between inequality and rising rates of labour unrest, mental illness, alcoholism and suicide.

THE CAUSES OF POVERTY

There is no mystery about why so many Canadians are relatively poor. The level of social assistance paid to families on welfare is in most cases below the poverty line. The minimum wages paid to the working poor are, as the Senate Committee said, "poverty wages." The federal and provincial welfare ministers, meeting in 1975, released a joint study by their officials on Income Support and Supplementation which provides revealing figures. For a family of two adults and two children in July 1974, the national average of social assistance paid by provincial governments, plus federal family allowance, was $4,041. The lowest poverty line at that time was over $5,000, and the Senate line was well over $7,000. Even the wealthiest provinces do not provide enough to lift a family out of poverty.

The heads of many poor families are not on welfare; they

work. But the national average minimum wage in 1974 was $2.11 an hour. A person who worked forty hours a week, fifty weeks in the year at that rate, and drew family allowances for two children, had an income of $4,700. Again, the family was below the poverty line.

So what happened to the truly enormous sums of money being spent on the famous welfare state, with its cradle-to-grave security, which was supposed to abolish poverty? The answer is that most of the money is being paid not to the poor, but to the middle and upper income groups. Family allowances, for example, are paid to rich and poor alike. So are the old age security pensions. And unemployment insurance benefits are available at a higher rate to the unemployed executive than to the seasonal labourer. The federal-provincial study estimated that $11.4 billion was being spent in 1974-75 on direct payments to support personal incomes. But of this huge sum, about $2.5 billion was allocated to the universal old age pension, $1.9 billion to family allowances, and $2.2 billion for unemployment benefits. Other substantial sums were accounted for by the contributory Canada Pension Plan, Workmen's Compensation, veterans' and survivors' pensions, assistance to native peoples, allowances for those taking Manpower training, student loans, and other schemes. Only about $2 billion went to what would commonly be regarded as welfare – that is, social assistance and other programs under the Canada Assistance Plan. Another $1 billion, approximately, was committed to the guaranteed income supplement to the old age pension for those without private income.

Governments also spend heavily on programs that are of indirect benefit to the poor. Federal "equalization" grants enable the less-developed provinces, in which incomes and tax revenues are below the national average, to provide a better level of public services than they could otherwise afford. Federal and provincial development grants encourage industry to locate in areas of high unemployment and low income. While sharing with the provinces the cost of hospital insurance and medicare, the federal government has rigged the formula so that it is more generous to low-income provinces. But all these and many other programs are also of benefit to middle and upper income groups and do not correct the imbalance in incomes. This is not to say they are

130

of no value to the poor; without them the poor would be much worse off, indeed in desperate straits. Families receiving less than $3,000 annually get 71 per cent of their income from government. The federal-provincial study estimated that without programs providing direct support to personal incomes, 36 per cent of families would be below the Senate poverty levels.

As we have seen, however, all these programs do not succeed in even maintaining the share of national income going to the poor. They barely keep the low income groups afloat in a rising tide of general affluence. In a speech in the Upper House in 1976, Senator David Croll, a lifelong crusader for improved social welfare, bemoaned the failure of public programs to bring about greater equality of income and produced a table of figures showing the limited impact of public spending on low incomes. Prepared in a government department and entitled "Impact of Tax, Transfer and Expenditure Policies of Government on the Distribution of Personal Income in Canada," the study estimated that in 1970, before any form of government intervention, the share of income going to the poorest 40 per cent of families was 16.7 per cent. After government intervention the share rose to 23.6 per cent. Between 1970 and 1973, there was a large increase in public spending on health and welfare programs, but according to the model, it raised the share of income only fractionally to 23.9 per cent. "Clearly," said Croll, "the . . . goal of government to provide a more equitable distribution of income has, so far, failed."

PROBLEMS OF REFORM

There is powerful resistance to any attempt to reform the systems of taxing and spending to make them more equitable. In 1970, the federal government published a White Paper, *Income Security for Canadians*, which proposed to reorganize family allowances and old age pensions to reduce payments to those not in need in order to increase payments to the poor. For example, it suggested doubling family allowances for families with incomes below $4,500 a year, scaling them down according to income for those in the $4,500 to $10,000 bracket, and stopping payments to those above $10,000. The result would have been to narrow the income gap, but there was strong opposition in the House of

Commons. Many argued that payments based upon income would identify the poor to their neighbours, and many MPs insisted upon maintaining the principle of universality – that is, equal allowances for all. The legislation failed to pass the Commons before the 1972 election.

After the election, the government was in a minority, and the price of survival in the House was to produce a new plan acceptable to one or more of the Opposition parties. Accordingly, it raised allowances for all families, regardless of income. The low income families got a bigger raise than they would have under the original scheme, but the middle and upper income classes got the same raise, so the gap was not narrowed. The total cost was, of course, very heavy. The fact that the allowances were made taxable as income effected some redistribution, because middle and high income earners pay a higher rate of tax than poor people. But the tax system is far from fully progressive – that is, based upon the principle of ability to pay – and the failure to reform it is another example of the resistance to change and social justice.

Prime Minister John Diefenbaker appointed a Royal Commission on Taxation (the Carter Commission) in 1962, mostly to placate the business community which believed, curiously, that it was overtaxed. The commission did a splendid job of research and analysis which revealed the inequities of the tax system, and proposed radical reform. The central principle of the new system came to be described in the amusing phrase, "A buck is a buck is a buck." It meant that however a dollar was acquired – in wages, by inheritance, in capital gain on the stock market, by gambling, even by finding it on the street – it should be taxed at the same rate. That would have increased tax on some of the ways in which the rich acquire and preserve their wealth – for example, by inheritance.

The Trudeau government modified Carter's proposals in a White Paper which was sent to committees of the Commons and Senate for examination. By the time the provincial governments, the farmers, the business associations, and other special interest groups had completed their barrage of criticism, government and Parliament were ready to dilute the reforms once again, and so the tax system remains unjust.

132

Taxes still weigh more heavily on lower income groups than they do on the rich. "When we look at taxes we find that, in 1969, the Canadian tax system was extremely regressive at the lower end of the income scale," said Economic Council chairman André Raynauld in 1973. "That is, the overall effective tax rates were higher for the poor than the rich."

Much of the opposition to social reform arises no doubt from the self-interest of the great majority of us who would have to give up part of our income in order to make more available to the poor. But to avoid facing the fact of our own selfishness we take refuge in myths.

The favourite myth is that the poor don't deserve help because they are a lazy lot who simply don't want to work. Study after study has shown this to be untrue. The Senate report noted that of the 832,000 families who fell below the poverty line in 1967, 525,000 had heads who were in the labour force, but working for poverty wages. The remainder were on welfare, said the committee, because they were not capable of earning a living: "They are the ones left behind by our economic system – the elderly, the sick, the disabled, and women in charge of families which require their presence in the home." In a study of *People and Jobs* published in 1976, the Economic Council repeated:

> The vast majority of welfare recipients are not employable. Half are permanently handicapped through chronic illness, disability, or old age; one third are unable to work because of temporary illness or because a spouse is absent and children must be cared for. Not more than one quarter of the recipients would be available for employment if jobs and adequate supporting services were available. The number rises and falls with economic conditions and includes workers who have exhausted their unemployment insurance benefits and others who are marginal farmers or farm workers who live in remote areas. Virtually all of these employable recipients work for some periods, but mostly in very marginal or short-term jobs.

The myth of the lazy and undeserving poor is kept alive and respectable because the focus of political criticism and media publicity is upon the relatively few cases of welfare abuse – the exceptions rather than the rule of the system.

133

Another myth is that the burden of taxation to support extravagant public spending is already so high and rising that we cannot afford to pay more without crippling the consumer and bankrupting business. The truth is that despite inflation and taxation, disposable incomes have been rising rapidly through the postwar years, and that it is government spending to sustain consumer demand that has made possible the expansion of private business. As we have seen, most government spending on social programs is recycled to the middle and upper income classes, and the impact of taxation is greatly exaggerated. Health and Welfare Minister Marc Lalonde pointed out that income tax paid by the wealthiest 20 per cent of Canadian families in 1971 reduced their share of total income by only 2 per cent. After paying income tax, the top 20 per cent still had 38 per cent of all income.

On the other hand, critics on the left like to claim that the real villains are the corporations and their profits. But, as the Carter report on taxation said, corporations are made up of people – people who own them, people who work for them, people who sell supplies to them, and people who buy from them. A tax on a corporation is a tax on some or all of these people. In order to pay the higher tax, the corporation may simply raise its prices, in which case the customer actually pays. Or it may require its employees to work harder for the same wages, in which case the worker pays. Or it may squeeze the price it pays to smaller companies that sell it goods and services, thus making them pay the tax. Even forcing it to pay the tax out of profit and reduce its dividend to the owners will only raise the price it has to pay for new capital in the future. In time, this new cost will be passed along to customers, workers, or suppliers. In practice, of course, the process of taxing corporation earnings is more complex than this, and it is possible in the short term to siphon off corporation profits. But in the long term, profits are a cost of doing business, in the same way as wages and raw materials are. Unless profits are maintained at a reasonable level, there is no incentive to invest and expand.

The best way to tax business earnings is not as corporation profit, but when they pass from the corporation to the shareholders, in the form of dividends or a rise in the value of stocks. But it would be a mistake to imagine there is any great reservoir of hidden profit to be tapped. A study by the Graduate School of Business at the University of Chicago, reported in *Fortune Magazine,* showed that for stock market investors the decade 1965-75 was the worst in half a century in the United States, and the story would be much the same in Canada. One dollar invested in the shares of a major U.S. corporation in 1965, with dividends faithfully reinvested for ten years, was worth 80 cents in 1975, after allowing for inflation. In the same period, the real value of earned income – wages and salaries – rose substantially, and from the proliferation of luxurious hotels and high-price restaurants, it appears that business executives, as distinct from owners, are enjoying expense-account living on a scale that is extravagant, although probably not significant in terms of national income.

There remain the great private fortunes, and there has been talk in Britain of taxing this wealth, as distinct from annual income. But to prevent the flight of capital from one country to another, it would probably be necessary for all the democracies to act more or less together to impose such a levy. Even then it would be foolhardy to use private capital to pay for current expenditures on social programs, for where then would we find capital for investment?

The myths provide no escape in the end from the reality that most of the funds required to raise the incomes of the poor will have to come from the middle income classes – probably in the form of wage and salary increases forgone rather than net reduction. There are certainly a few thousand Canadians who enjoy very high incomes and ought in equity to pay more tax. But even if all their incomes were cut in half, the total of revenue would not be impressive. The National Revenue department analyses tax returns every year, and its most recent report showed that in 1974 only 6,745 people had an income before tax of more than $100,000, for a total of $875 million. All 8.9 million taxpayers reported incomes totalling just under $90 billion. Of these, 61 per cent received an income of $10,000 or less totalling about $33 billion; 38 per cent received an income between $10,000 and $50,-000, totalling about $52 billion. Less than one per cent received an income of more than $50,000, for a total of about $4 billion. In summary, the big money to be taxed is in the middle income range.

135

GUARANTEED INCOME

A quarter century of economic growth and rapid expansion of the welfare state has raised the living standards of the entire country, including the poor. But the income gap between the poor and the middle and upper income groups has widened in the same period. It is clear, therefore, that we cannot rely on growth, even if it continues, or on existing social welfare programs, to solve the problem of relative poverty. We need a new mechanism that will raise the incomes of the poor above the poverty line and guarantee to keep them in step, at least, with the rise in the general level of incomes: a guaranteed income program.

The concept of guaranteeing incomes is not revolutionary. In fact, we already have several such programs. Family allowances guarantee a minimum income for families with children. Old age security guarantees a minimum for pensioners. Social assistance guarantees a minimum for those on welfare. In a more general sense, we guarantee that no one in our society will die because he or she has insufficient income to obtain food and shelter. All that remains to be done to abolish poverty is to raise the level of the guaranteed income above the poverty line and to devise a more efficient mechanism for getting the money to those in need. It is a matter of political will and technique.

Technique is relatively easy. Various models of a guaranteed income plan are available; one of the most popular, negative income tax, has been described by the National Council of Welfare in this way:

> In its broadest terms, the idea behind the negative income tax is to round out the income tax system so that it not only collects money from higher income families but also provides benefits to lower income families. As is well known, under the existing tax system each family is allowed a certain amount of exempt income upon which taxes are not paid; there are exemptions for the taxpayer, his or her spouse, and each of their children. If a family's income exceeds the exemption level, then the family pays taxes to the government. If its income is less than the exemption level, the family doesn't pay taxes. The existing tax system does redistribute income since it takes more money from higher income families, and less

money (or none at all) from lower income families. But it doesn't provide any *additional* money to those at the bottom of the income scale. The family whose income is below the exemption level for a family of its size doesn't have to pay any taxes, but neither does this family get any benefits back from the government through the tax system. A negative income tax would go beyond this existing system by providing benefits to families with incomes below the exemption level. The level of benefits would depend on family size and income. Larger families would get more than smaller families. As a family's income decreased, the level of benefits would increase.

In short, income tax as we know it taxes away a proportion of income from those who have wages and salaries, but does nothing for the poor who have little or no income. A negative income tax would pay income to those unable to earn for themselves. Such a scheme could replace some but not all the many welfare programs now in existence. There would be difficult administrative problems, no doubt, but in concept it would be neat and fair, working more or less automatically to raise the incomes of all the poor above the pre-determined poverty line.

The problem of mobilizing the political will and the financial resources to pay for a generous guaranteed income is much more serious. The federal government has been trying to persuade the provincial governments to co-operate in launching a modest program for some time, but the provinces have balked. The provincial politicians probably reflect public opinion in this matter more accurately than the federal politicians. Canadians are said to be in a conservative mood, worried about slow growth in the economy combined with inflation and unemployment, persuaded their taxes are too high, disillusioned because the welfare state has not performed as promised, and convinced they are being ripped-off by both the poor and the rich. They are not willing to take on major new social commitments, despite the numerous reports that have documented the poverty problem and the commitment in principle of all parties to find a solution.

An effective way to bring the public to face the issue and to change its attitude would be to establish the economic policy forum suggested in the previous chapter. The public and private interest groups meeting in public to discuss the economic outlook and to debate the competing claims on resources would have to take account of the claims of the poor, expressed by the federal government in its proposed guaranteed income program. The claim would have to be weighed against others, for higher wages, fatter profits, more generous farm subsidies, new investment in business which might or might not be of high priority, other forms of government expenditure, and so on. It is hard to believe the claims of the poor could be long denied in a rational, public debate about the allocation of new wealth in our affluent society. But if funds were committed to a guaranteed income program, there would have to be a corresponding saving elsewhere in the economy. Money might be diverted to a guaranteed income scheme by holding down the natural rise in earned incomes and salaries, by means of a special tax, or by keeping the current anti-inflation controls on incomes in place for a year or two. In fact, a national agreement to make modest sacrifices in order to achieve the national goal of abolishing poverty might well prove popular at a time when Canadians are said to be weary of consumerism and seeking a meaning and purpose in their lives.

In summary, we ought to have an incomes policy that not only seeks to curb the demand for private affluence in the form of rising wages and profits, but also recognizes the claim of the poor to a fairer share of the national income.

7

The Worker

The new society will have to change the concept and organization of work to meet the demands of the new worker and the
needs of the new economy. The master-servant era in which
workers were kept subservient to authoritarian employers by
feelings of social inferiority and fear of unemployment is already
long behind us. We are in a period in which the employer is boss
rather than master, still with power, prestige, and privilege, but
expected by society to be humane in his treatment of labour,
forced by unions to negotiate on wages and conditions, and faced
by workers who are protected from economic disaster by the
social security net. In the new era we are now entering the
worker demands equality with the boss (or something close to it),
job satisfaction as well as wages, and a voice in the management
of the business. Citizens who have been taught to reject arbitrary
political power and who refuse to accept traditional social class
distinctions are naturally questioning also the sources of
authority in the workplace. They are seeking some form of
democracy in industry that will give them greater control over
the environment in which they spend so much of their lives.

The new attitude to work and employment arises from other
changes in society. Probably the most important factor is the
increase in the number of young people in the labour force. In
People and Jobs, a study of the Canadian labour market published in 1976, the Economic Council remarked cautiously:

What is particularly noteworthy about the large component of our total labour force represented by young people is that their patterns of behaviour and their attitudes towards work tend to be different from those of the older members of the population. From the evidence, it seems reasonable to hypothesize that for those who have no children or other family responsibilities, or who may be able to depend on their parents for financial support, there is less concern about the continuity of earnings that steady employment provides.Thus they can more readily leave jobs they do not enjoy or take work they know will not last very long. This relatively relaxed attitude towards security of work may lead some to countenance unemployment more readily than is possible for those with families to support.

That is no doubt true, but one can go much further in explaining the attitudes of the young. They are the children of an affluent society who have grown up in an expanding economy without the fearful experience of the Great Depression which conditioned their grandparents and shadowed their parents. They are better informed than previous generations, at least in the sense that they know enough popular sociology and economics to question the pretensions of their superiors at work. Through their school teachers or as university students they have been introduced to the social analysis of such influential academics as C. Wright Mills *(The Power Elite)* and John Porter *(The Vertical Mosaic),* and to the economic criticism of Marx, Galbraith, and more orthodox theoreticians. They have watched the mass media questioning the legitimacy of government and of business corporations, and in their own homes they have been subject to less parental discipline and socializing than previous generations. In a world in which money is relatively easy to come by and technology seems to make everything possible, they are short on patience and long on expectations.

A second important change is the increasing number of women in the labour force. Some are driven to work by economic necessity, but many are seeking new experiences outside the home. As the Economic Council noted, social and cultural developments "have altered women's perceptions of their role in society, which, coupled with more effective birth-control methods, have led to reduced emphasis on child-bearing and to greater career orientation." The modern woman worker is less submissive than her mother and more ambitious. As an occasional worker seeking to supplement the family income or to find a new interest after her children have grown up, she adds flexibility to the work force, distorting the familiar statistics of employment and unemployment. As a full-time worker pursuing a career, she has increased the competition for jobs and, perhaps, brought new ideas and attitudes to traditional preserves of the male.

The youth revolution, so-called, and the women's movement are only part of a wider change toward a more democratic and permissive society in which most people have modified their values, including their attitudes to work. Because travel, education and training for new careers are more readily available than ever before, there is a general tendency to be less formal in working relationships, less respectful of authority, less bound by a rigid sense of duty, less settled in routine. It may be true that there is now a reaction against some aspects of the permissive society, a desire to return to a more structured way of life, but this is not likely to have much effect on how the new worker views his or her job. Over the next few years, the proportion of young and women workers in the labour force is expected to continue to increase rapidly, and the Economic Council forecasts, "By 1985 half of the young people leaving school to take permanent jobs will have at least some postsecondary education, along with the aspirations that accompany such training."

A fourth factor in shaping attitudes has been the reluctant but growing realization that the private sector of the economy can produce all the goods and services we need and more, without employing all those who wish to work. Even in boom times with industry producing to capacity, the national level of unemployment has been disturbingly high. If, as some responsible authorities believe, we are now entering an era of slower growth, perhaps even zero growth, the problem will become more serious in the future. A society concerned to conserve natural resources and protect the environment will have to limit the production of new consumer goods and services, thereby restricting the creation of new jobs.

141

We are beginning to see that some years ago our view of work and production underwent a subtle distortion. Where formerly the object of work had been the production of goods and services to meet genuine need, we came to accept that the object of production was to provide employment. Public policy stimulated industry to grow by creating new products and services not because they were needed by consumers, but because there was thought to be a need for the work entailed in producing them. Few people stopped to consider that if society could meet all its reasonable needs for goods and services without employing all the available labour, the answer might be to encourage more paid leisure or public service in one form or another. That idea is now taking hold, and many young people are asking why they should be expected to employ their minds and bodies producing goods and services which consume energy and other limited resources, but are of only dubious value to consumers.

THE WORK ETHIC

These new attitudes seeping through the economic system have caused some to fear that the work ethic is dying; that is, that young people are no longer prepared to seek satisfaction in hard labour. As the work ethic is often identified with the rise of capitalism and liberal democracy, a decline in the ethic may seem to predict economic and political disaster. But this is to misunderstand what is changing. People still want to work; they simply want to work at more satisfying jobs. The Economic Council concluded:

> All the evidence [from its own research] ... and the findings reported in several recent studies of Canadian work values, indicated that Canadians are strongly motivated to work and generally hold jobs not only because they have to, but because they like to. According to these studies, Canadians as a people regard work as the main vehicle to success, broadly defined; in terms of personal satisfaction and self-fulfilment, they rank work second only to family, or sometimes friendship, ties. ...
> The surveys confirm the importance of pay, advancement, and fringe benefits as fundamental factors in the decision to accept a job. But, once in a job, the greatest personal satisfaction

seems to derive from having enough authority and information to work effectively, from friendly co-workers and supervisors, and from interesting assignments with visible results from one's efforts.

Bonnie Campbell, reporting in the *Labour Gazette,* official journal of the federal Department of Labour, on the 1973 Couchiching Conference organized by the Canadian Institute on Public Affairs, said:

> One consensus that emerged from the conference was that the young are increasingly demanding jobs that are more than a source of income; they want personal satisfaction. This demand manifests itself in many ways, including a marked distaste for dreary, routine work; demands for more democracy in the work place and more responsibility for the quality of the end product, and often a preference for work that will be socially useful or significant.

This does not suggest a retreat from work and social responsibility; rather the opposite. A task force reporting to the u.s. Secretary of Health, Education and Welfare in 1973 on "Work in America," said:

> Work offers economic self-sufficiency, status, family stability, and an opportunity to interact with others in one of the most basic activities of society. Consequently, if the opportunity to work is absent or if the nature of work is dissatisfying (or worse), severe repercussions are likely to be experienced in other parts of the social system. And significant numbers of American workers are dissatisfied with the quality of their working lives. Dull, repetitive, seemingly meaningless tasks, offering little challenge or autonomy, are causing discontent among workers at all occupational levels. This is not so much because work itself has greatly changed; indeed, one of the main problems is that work has not changed fast enough to keep up with the rapid and widescale changes in worker attitudes, aspirations, and values. A general increase in their educational and economic status has placed many American workers in a position where having an interesting job is now as important as having a job that pays well.

The task force commissioned a number of specific studies and reviewed research by others to conclude: "What the workers want most, as more than 100 studies in the past 20 years show, is to become masters of their immediate environments and to feel that their work and they themselves are important – the twin ingredients of self-esteem."

Abraham Maslow, in *Motivation and Personality* as quoted by the task force, suggested that as human beings achieve one level of satisfaction, another becomes the goal. He said the first requirements were physiological – food, housing, etc.; the second were for safety and security; the third for companionship and affection; the fourth for self-esteem and the esteem of others; and the fifth for self-actualization – being able to realize one's potential. It appears that the success of the capitalist system in providing food, shelter, security, and a degree of freedom of lifestyle has encouraged us to raise our sights and to seek now the esteem of the boss and work that tests the limits of capacity. Only an economic depression or other disaster that reduced the standard of living and destroyed security, pushing our achievement down a level or two, could turn us back from the new goals which we seek in work.

These new goals represent not a dramatic revolution, but another stage on the long march to escape the tyranny of unrelieved and unrewarding toil. For whatever Protestant divines may have preached about the spiritual value of labour, there have always been forms of work that could not be regarded as ends in themselves, satisfying to the labourer. Most societies – even Plato's ideal Republic – have needed slaves driven by the lash or by harsh economic necessity to do the menial work. Through history, it has been the consistent aim of enlightened leaders to reduce the burden of work, by shortening hours, improving conditions, introducing machines to replace men. Most such reforms have been resisted by conservatives fearful of change in any form, and often they have come about only when workers have revolted against conditions of labour, or when employers have seen the opportunity to make profits. Adapting to the new attitudes and expectations will be no easier in the new society than it was in the past for it will require us once again to change the way in which we think about work and jobs and unemployment and how we regard the rights of the employer and the employee. Let us now look at each of these subjects.

GUARANTEED WORK

With reservations, the Economic Council, in its report on *People and Jobs,* defined work as "paid employment." But, as the U.S. task force pointed out, that is unsatisfactory and indeed absurd. A woman who is paid to keep house for another family is recognized as a worker contributing to the Gross National Product, but if the same woman does the same work for her own family, she is not a worker. A handyman who works to build a house for sale is a worker, but when he builds a house for his own family, he is not a worker. Volunteers providing social services to the community are not paid, but they certainly work – sometimes harder than those in paid employment. Students who elect to improve their education in order to work more effectively in future, instead of going directly into an unskilled job, are certainly working although they actually pay fees instead of earning wages.

When we define work in a broad sense we realize there is no shortage of work in our society. Business may not be able to provide work and wages for everybody seeking employment, and may have difficulty making jobs satisfying, but there is a constant demand for new and better public services, often at the community level. For example, when the federal government invited young people to invent jobs for themselves under the Opportunities for Youth program, it was flooded with imaginative proposals. As usual, political criticism and media publicity focused on the failures and the few outright frauds, but the great majority of projects were at least partly successful and eventually achieved social acceptance in most communities. The Local Initiatives Program extended the same job-inventing technique to the adult unemployed and achieved a similar success. Ministers seeking a political sacrifice to dramatize their determination to save money eventually cancelled the OFY scheme and curtailed LIP. But the concept of guaranteeing community service work for those who can't obtain jobs in the private sector, or find them unsatisfying, is gradually gaining acceptance.

A number of proposals for guaranteeing work have been made. Among them, three stand out. First we have the National Council of Welfare's suggestion that the definition of "work" be expanded:

> We have not yet adjusted our thinking to the notion that a job need not be unpleasant, that it need not involve the production of a commercial product. We still cling to the idea that activities such as undoing the results of pollution, providing services to senior citizens and improving the quality of neighbourhood life are somehow unproductive forms of employment while putting the caps on bottles of underarm deodorant instead of letting a machine do it represents a contribution to the nation's economic growth. ... There are no limits to our freedom to recognize as meaningful activity any sort of activity which is meaningful to us. A program of guaranteed jobs through a redefinition of our concept of a job could entirely eliminate what we now call unemployment. And it could encompass many of those whom we now regard as unemployable; because they are unemployable only in terms of the traditional, narrow definition of employment.

A second suggestion came from the government itself, which proposed in its *Working Paper on Social Security in Canada* establishment of a community employment program:

> Its purpose would be to provide socially useful employment to people who have been unemployed for an extended period of time, either by reason of the lack of jobs in the areas in which they might reasonably be expected to look for work, or by reason of the "employability" of the people concerned.

The idea would be to make grants available to voluntary agencies, "local initiative" groups, and probably to local governments. Unfortunately, the provincial governments were more interested in controlling the costs of existing social programs than in starting new ones, and the federal scheme was reduced to a few experimental projects.

The Economic Council took up the same theme in its study, *People and Jobs:*

> In the course of carrying out this study, we have been

impressed by two things. First, although in the large metropolitan areas and cities the average rates of unemployment are lower than in most smaller communities, in absolute numbers most of the unemployed are living in or around cities. Second, it is in these same cities and metropolitan areas that there is a real need for better police protection, better health care, pollution control, industrial safety, recreational activity, transportation facilities and the like, and where the tax base simply does not provide fully for these services. In short, unmet needs and idle human beings coexist. With a suitable catalyst, they might well be conjoined productively. By the same token, taxes that are now channeled to unemployment insurance claimants might well be more efficiently used to create jobs that help to meet recognized common needs.

The council proposed to divert about $1 billion a year from unemployment insurance to create between 100,000 and 200,000 jobs in the public service sector. They would be permanent positions, but available only for short periods to people temporarily unable to find regular jobs.

While the National Council of Welfare, the federal working paper and the Economic Council were all talking about creating work in the public sector, they had rather different objectives. The National Council was seeking to make a guaranteed income program more acceptable by linking it to the concept of guaranteed jobs. By redefining work to include many occupations that do not now attract earnings, it could justify paying a public wage. The federal plan was much more cautious and aimed only at the long-term unemployed. Indeed, Health and Welfare Minister Marc Lalonde was concerned that a broad program of community employment would draw more workers into the labour force, and perhaps even attract labour to leave private industry for lower-paying but more satisfying community work. The Economic Council, on the other hand, proposed an ambitious program, but open only to those temporarily disengaged from the private sector. The important point, however, is that all recognized the principle of providing public employment for those unable to find conventional jobs. As the public comes to understand that unemployment cannot be reduced by conventional methods, the consensus on the need for some form of guaranteed job scheme will grow over the next few years.

One can add a fourth concept to those described above. The military has often been a heavy employer of young people. In some countries, conscription is customary; in others, including Canada, young volunteers have marched away to war in most generations. Although it is conventional to speak of war in terms of horror, the truth is that for many young men it has been a way of escape from home, to find adventure and test one's mettle in new surroundings among new friends from different walks of life. In the absence of a major war in the past quarter-century, we have seen attempts, official and unofficial, to invent alternative occupations. The Company of Young Canadians and Canadian University Service Overseas are two of the best-known official "service corps." Paradoxically, the anti-nuclear and anti-war demonstrations in Europe and North America had a military flavour. They were described as "marches"; the leaders sometimes spoke in terms of "the spring offensive," or "the winter campaign," the young people often dressed in war-surplus clothing, and in any event, jeans were clearly a uniform; the more radical among them eagerly studied manuals of guerrilla warfare.

As there appears to be a strong desire among the young in their late teens and early twenties to join their peers in mass organizations directed to common goals, it would be a good idea to establish a public service corps and conscript the young to serve in it for a year or two. Many Canadians may object to the idea of conscription, but education is compulsory, so why not a couple of extra years of service on leaving school? Conscription would demand equal service from all, and not merely from the underprivileged. Such an organization could provide labour for public services, from hospitals to armed forces. There would also be an opportunity to raise standards of fitness, repair defects in basic education, improve the knowledge of current affairs and counsel the young on opportunities for further education and careers in a more intensive way than is possible in school.

The cost of all these community employment programs no doubt deters many people. But as we noted in the previous chapter, we already provide a minimum income in some form to all those who cannot support themselves through regular employment. The proposal to guarantee a job is essentially to offer these

148

people an opportunity to "work for their welfare." As we have discussed, this could be done in part by redefining work. For example, the single mother could be assigned to look after her children (who would otherwise be in subsidized daycare centres or perhaps wards of a children's aid society) and paid a wage rather than welfare. The young could be put to work in a service corps at a weekly wage instead of drifting in and out of subsidized education and collecting unemployment insurance. Adults unable to find a place in private industry could be found useful work in public service, or paid to attend university, or subsidized to develop an artistic talent, instead of drawing unemployment benefits, or welfare assistance. The returns to society would more than outweigh the additional cost on top of the money already being spent to replace or supplement incomes obtained from conventional employment.

The question for the new society is only how fast we wish to proceed on this great reform. Meantime, we have to revise our out-dated ideas about unemployment in the private sector and the operations of the unemployment insurance scheme.

UNEMPLOYMENT

The great depression of the 1930s produced mass unemployment, material hardship, and mental suffering among those who felt rejected and useless. There was also the knowledge that the failure to employ labour and resources meant a failure to produce goods and services in a needy country, indeed a needy world. When it became generally realized during and after the Second World War that unemployment had been the result of insufficient demand in the economy arising from incompetent management by government, there was an almost unanimous resolve not to let such a disaster happen again. Canada and other industrial democracies undertook to maintain full employment – which was usually interpreted to mean not more than 3 per cent of the labour force out of work. This 3 per cent comprised those changing jobs, temporarily laid off, or more or less unemployable by reason of mental or physical defect.

The failure to achieve full employment in the fifties and sixties was usually ascribed to the stupidity of governors who did not know enough to apply Keynesian techniques, or to the cruelty of

149

politicians who were suspected of being in league with Big Business to grind the faces of the poor and ensure a supply of cheap labour. These ideas were held so strongly that, as we have seen in an earlier chapter, unemployment was still being interpreted as proof of insufficient demand in the seventies when, in fact, rising demand and expectations were already generating severe inflation.

We now have to get away from the idea that short-term unemployment is necessarily bad, an indication of weakness in the economy and of widespread suffering. The national statistics of unemployment are not a reliable guide to demand in the economy because they reflect regional circumstances. While industrial centres are experiencing full employment – or even overfull employment with not enough workers to fill available jobs – the less-developed regions, where jobs depend on the season, may have high unemployment, pushing up the national average. Any attempt to stimulate the economy by cutting taxes or increasing spending may merely increase demand in industry, causing inflation, while doing little for the unemployed.

The gross rate of unemployment is unsatisfactory also because it does not distinguish between different classes of workers. For example, the high level of unemployment among the young, which distorts the average, results in part from the fact that young people tend to experiment with various jobs, and to take holidays between jobs, before settling down.

The unemployment rate no longer measures hardships in realistic terms because, as the Economic Council reported, only about one-third of those drawing unemployment insurance benefits are primary breadwinners for a family. One half are supplementary breadwinners – that is, they are members of a family in which at least one other person is employed – and one-eighth are unattached individuals responsible only for their own welfare.

Unemployment insurance and other forms of social security not only relieve hardship, but also actually encourage people to give up their jobs for one reason or another. An Economic Council study estimated that, on the average during 1972 and 1973, there were 100,000 to 150,000 persons unemployed because it was easier to draw benefits than to stay at work or find a job.

150

They were not, of course, always the same people. Workers move in and out of employment, and during 1973, for example, over two million Canadians drew benefits. Some undoubtedly were cheating – taking advantage of administrative defects in the new scheme to secure benefits to which they were not really entitled under the regulations – but the great majority were law-abiding citizens.

Nevertheless, there has been much public criticism, echoed and magnified by the media, at the very idea of "induced" unemployment – of workers drawing insurance benefits when they could have been employed. This is a narrow view because there have always been large numbers of people who have been able to live at the expense of the community without working, or without working very hard. The idle rich have always been with us, living on capital accumulated by their forebears. Wives of successful men often exist comfortably with a minimum of labour, employing servants, or services such as laundries and restaurants and babysitters and later boarding schools, to look after domestic chores and family responsibilities. Upper-class young people have usually been allowed extended vacations. Although these may appear to be private extravagances, at some point the cost falls on the economy.

So in one sense, unemployment insurance merely relieves the pressure of work on ordinary Canadians, enabling them to enjoy a more middle-class lifestyle. In another sense, it may improve productivity. The Economic Council study recognized both these factors in the conclusion about the level of induced unemployment. An increase in unemployment, it said, is not necessarily a reflection of an unhealthy economy:

> It may be an indicator of increasing affluence as well as an indicator of improvement in worker "welfare," rather than the opposite. In other words, if increased wealth per family unit, multi-earner families, and unemployment insurance now allow the typical labour force participant to be choosier before accepting employment, then participants, we would argue, are "better off" even if their lengthened duration of unemployment tends to increase the unemployment rate. While society may lose some output which would have been produced if unemployment was less, this "welfare loss" may be offset by

increased worker satisfaction in job choice and perhaps even in higher productivity.

In summary, the keepers of the conventional wisdom in Parliament, the trade unions, and the media have been slow to recognize that unemployment, far from being a true measure of hardship, is to some degree a measure of the opposite – of the extent to which people are able to take a break from work they do not enjoy and to take longer in searching for a new job in which they will find satisfaction and be able to work with enthusiasm and efficiency.

INDUSTRIAL DEMOCRACY

To the employer in the free market, labour is a factor of production, like machines and raw materials, to be bought as cheaply as possible and worked as hard as possible to yield the greatest profit. In small enterprises, the boss may have a paternal concern for the welfare of his staff; in large companies, the manager is usually forced to sign a contract with his workers' union. Enlightened employers realize that well paid and relatively contented workers are likely to be more productive and therefore more profitable than cheap and resentful labourers. But the central fact remains that the employer hires, fires, and directs labour according to his own judgement of his best interest, while the worker tips his hat and does as he is told, or tries to find a better job. In short, the relationship of the boss to the worker is authoritarian.

In a society that professes to be democratic in other respects, this arrangement is justified by what are known as the "rights of property," and on grounds of efficiency. It is reasoned that if a man saves his money, or takes the risk of borrowing from others, to start a business, he must be allowed to run it as he sees fit, establishing the conditions of work and hiring and firing, subject only to laws governing safety and minimum wages and to whatever contract he may make with his workers. Because his own money is at stake, he will run the business efficiently, which means providing a product at a price consumers will pay. The right of the worker, on the other hand, is only to sell his labour for the best price he can get.

Nobody can question the efficiency of the system in the sense that it has mobilized capital, labour, and resources to expand production at an extraordinary rate to satisfy the demand in industrial democracies not only for material necessities, but also for luxuries. But the system is increasingly being challenged on the ground that it does not satisfy the demand for a better quality of life.

We have noted in previous chapters the demand in democratic societies for more participation in political decision-making and for greater economic equality. With more education and a stronger sense of social security, people are questioning traditional relationships between the governors and the governed, the rich and the less-rich. The same questioning attitudes are naturally appearing in the workplace. Workers who are assured they are free men and women with an inalienable right to choose their government are asking why they should submit to the dictatorship of the boss. Workers who have submitted to the tyranny of the production line or the office bureaucracy to achieve a high material standard of life are now seeking work that recognizes their dignity as persons and provides an opportunity to be creative. According to *Work in America:*

The more democratic and self-affirmative an individual is, the less he will stand for boring, dehumanized and authoritarian work. Under such conditions, the workers either protest or give in, at some cost to their psychological well-being. Anger that does not erupt may be frozen into schizoid depressed characters who escape into general alienation, drugs and fantasies. More typically, dissatisfying work environments result in the condition known as alienation. Alienation exists when workers are unable to control their immediate work processes, to develop a sense of purpose and function which connects their jobs to the over-all organization of production, to belong to integrated industrial communities, or when they fail to become involved in the activity of work as a mode of self-expression.

One of the most dramatic demonstrations of dissatisfaction occurred in 1972 when workers at a new, highly mechanized auto factory at Lordstown, Ohio, struck in protest against the in-

153

human demands of the production line. There has been no comparable outbreak in Canada, but a 1972 resolution from the Canadian council of the United Auto Workers declared:

> It is increasingly clear that the work in the assembly plants, i.e., automobile, aircraft, implements and parts, has become a critical problem because increasing numbers of workers find their work fundamentally dissatisfying and dehumanizing. The intrinsic physical nature of the assembly line denies man the opportunity to think about, let alone take pride in, his work. The assembly line alienates, bores, depersonalizes and dehumanizes. In the present terms, worker dissatisfaction is expressed in drugs, alcoholism, fury, and hopelessness.

The *Labour Gazette* published a statement by Dennis McDermott, Canadian director of the UAW, in 1973: "When young people go into the plant . . . they find themselves in an atmosphere that is completely foreign to their idea of freedom. . . . Some of the young people don't last more than two hours on the job; they just walk out. . . . The job is no longer the most valuable thing to them."

It is surely a reasonable assumption that the nature of work itself is one of the factors provoking strikes, both wildcat and official. A strike may be no more than an escape from boring routine, an assertion of freedom and independence from the dictates of the boss. Indeed, the rising incidence of strikes in Canada prompted increasing interest in European systems in which workers participate in management rather than being simple adversaries, and in experiments in Europe and North America in redesigning work and the working environment to make life in the factory and the office more acceptable. "To a greater extent than ever before, the question of whether workers should play a more important role in the decision-making process affecting jobs and the central issues of industrial production is being asked more persistently throughout all the industrial countries, and it is being raised by a broader cross-section of the public," acknowledged Donald MacDonald, then president of the Canadian Labour Congress in the CLC journal, *Canadian Labour,* in 1972.

It is, of course, one thing to ask questions, another to find answers, and a third to translate promising answers into working solutions. The U.S. task force recommended redesigning jobs to give workers more variety, independence, and scope for initiative. It described successful experiments by some of the largest corporations and concluded, "not only can work be redesigned to make it more satisfying, but that significant increases in productivity can also be obtained. In other words, workers can be healthier, happier in their work, and better contributors to family and community life than they are now, without a loss of goods and services, and without inflating prices." In some cases, workers were invited to help design their factory, choose their foreman, arrange working hours, swap jobs to break monotony – in fact, adopt any method they wished to meet the production and profit targets set by management. Profit sharing was proposed to avoid the suspicion that more efficient production meant merely more exploitation.

There has been much interest in Canada also in new auto plants in Sweden in which workers were organized in production teams to build a car from start to finish, instead of each repeating one function on a production line. If these systems prove to be successful in raising the satisfaction and productivity of workers we can be certain they will be adopted in time by profit-conscious employers in Canada, but at best they do not change the basic relationship between boss and worker.

At the other extreme of proposed solutions, so to speak, is the socialist theory that it is necessary to abolish private ownership to end the exploitation of the worker by the capitalist. Under public ownership, co-operation is supposed to replace competition; public service rather than private gain becomes the incentive to work; and all labour happily for the common good. But experience with Crown corporations and government departments has shown that state ownership and management may be no better than private ownership, and perhaps worse because the former lacks the incentive of profit to be efficient and innovative. State capitalism may be the least desirable of all systems. Other forms of non-private ownership – producer and consumer co-ops, for example – may be more successful, but as long as the great majority of businesses continue to be privately owned and to operate in a modified free market, public enterprises will be under pressure to compete by adopting the meth-

155

ods and criteria of private ownership.

It would be foolish also to ignore the evidence that man, as a part of his nature or as the result of long conditioning, is an acquisitive creature who responds to the profit incentive – that is, who works hardest to improve his own position. Certainly there have always been some persons apparently able to rise above the prospect of private gain and they have been widely admired, which suggests that we aspire to a motive for work higher than profit. But for the foreseeable future, the promise of private profit seems likely to be a more important incentive to productivity than the opportunity for public service.

Democratic socialists are inhibited also by the fact, already noted, that their trade union allies are part of the market system and suspicious of change. Union leaders are accustomed to view management as a natural adversary with whom they struggle to secure better wages and conditions for the workers. They are, therefore, inclined to view as unnatural any proposals that workers should share in management – partly no doubt because their own roles in the system might be diminished. NDP leader Ed Broadbent has been an enthusiastic advocate of industrial democracy. In his book, *The Liberal Rip-Off,* published in 1972, he said:

> I want to stress that industrial democracy as it relates to the work place is not an empty academic catch-phrase but a term to describe the involvement of the worker in his working life. Let me be precise on this point. It is not concerned with deceptive "happiness" techniques: Muzak, painted work areas, employee saunas, and the whole range of cunning devices by which employees are amused and distracted and whose purpose it is to maintain the status quo in decision-making authority. It is concerned with democratic rights and the human goals of self-respect and self-realization, with the ideal of personal fulfilment that is at the heart of socialism. The central human problem of modern industrialism is the alienation of the worker from his work.

But Broadbent seems to be reconciled to progress at a pace to be set by the unions. He urges unions to move beyond negotiation of wages and hours to bring within the collective bargaining

156

process "conditions related to the making of crucial decisions about production, about the allocation of capital, about the nature and price of products and about the distribution of profits." He may have to be patient. In *Jobs and People,* the Economic Council reported:

On the whole, organized labor has responded very cautiously to job experimentation or enrichment. This partly reflects the suspicion that experimentation would mask a process that would eliminate jobs or oblige employees to work at more demanding speeds or tasks than at present. And it may partly represent a healthy realism, since inevitably the very nature of some activities leads to impersonal, repetitive, or physically arduous jobs. In such instances, labor's approach has been to press for the highest possible earnings and fringe benefits, combined with sufficient leisure time to enjoy what the earning will provide. ... Similarly, Canadian unions have approached participation in managerial decision-making or participatory management very cautiously. Labor/management committees in Canada tend to serve as advisory or consultative bodies for the purpose of smoothing communications and helping to settle grievances and eliminate irritations, rather than as vehicles for joint management. Some years ago the CLC made a survey of European experiences with this technique. It approved, in principle, joint participation in decision-making on wages, working conditions, job security, and work methods, but it made clear that it preferred the traditional Canadian system to the newer industrial relations approaches being tried in other countries.

In the United States and to a lesser extent in Canada, there has been interest in schemes to make employees shareholders in the companies for which they work in order to give them a greater sense of participation and responsibility. A new U.S. tax law offers an incentive to companies to finance expansion by issuing to employees shares which then serve as security on which new capital can be borrowed. This plan has been described as a sort of peoples' capitalism, spreading the benefits of private enterprise. David Treleaven, a businessman and leader of the Committee for an Independent Canada, has suggested that a similar scheme here would, among other purposes, serve to encourage Canadian ownership and reduce foreign control. Some Canadian corporations already encourage employees to buy shares and participate in profits, although few expect them to acquire enough to obtain the power to interfere with management. A recent report from the United States claimed that through their pension funds, workers own at least 25 per cent of the private sector, and by 1985, will own 50 to 60 per cent. But pension funds are widely invested by professional managers and give the worker no particular sense of participation in the company for which he works. The worker also participates in profits through the tax on profits which the government spends for the general welfare, but again the worker has no particular reason to identify his benefits with the profitability of his own employer.

In West Germany and many other European democracies, the law insists that workers have representation on boards of directors. In fact, the German legislature extended the scheme in 1976 to ensure that workers will have more or less equal representation with shareholders on boards of companies with more than 2,000 employees. The boards are concerned with policy rather than day-to-day management, and there are different opinions about how much power the workers' directors really have and what benefits flow to the shopfloor. But the fact is that Austria, Norway, Denmark, and Holland have thought it wise to copy the German model to some extent, and Britain has been studying a similar scheme. In Canada, C.K. Marchant, an economist, public servant, and policy adviser to the Ontario government, proposed to the Royal Commission on Corporate Concentration in 1976 that not only workers but also consumers and representatives of the public interest should be assured seats on boards of directors. "These fundamental changes are proposed with two main objectives in mind," said Marchant in his brief. "First, in terms of corporate democracy, to give the large enterprise both a clearer mandate and a clearer responsibility to deal with the full range of consumer, employee, public and shareholder interests affected by its operations, practices and products. It is argued that this will strengthen the role of the individual enterprise in our society. Second, the proposal would eliminate the need for excessive government regulation designed to deal with corporate practices harmful to consumer, employee and public interests."

But while the purpose of such a reform might be to preserve corporate enterprise and resist government regulation, the effect would seem to be to weaken capitalism in the sense that corporations would be directed not primarily in the interests of capital – that is, the shareholders – but in the interests of workers, customers, and the wider society.

THE NEW WORKER

It is sometimes argued that workers don't really want to be bothered by industrial democracy. Their jobs are said to be unavoidably boring or even unpleasant, and the only realistic goal is to ensure they have to work as few hours as possible and have the monetary compensation to enjoy leisure. This view is no doubt correct to a considerable extent. Most workers, after all, don't bother to attend union meetings, and only a tiny fraction of the general public participates in politics between elections. But no one proposes to abolish unions or scrap democracy. They are, at the very least, a safety valve for dissatisfaction, a safeguard against oppression, and an assurance to the individual of his status. More democracy in industry would not automatically make work less boring, tiring, dirty, or even unhealthy. But it would begin to change the relationship between employer and employee from one of superior-inferior to one of greater equality and therefore of greater dignity. It would create the mechanism by which the other problems and conflicts in the workplace could be eased if not always resolved.

The new society will clearly have to move in this direction to meet the aspirations of the new workers, and it will probably be best to experiment with several different reforms. Corporations should be required to transfer a small percentage of profit each year to employees in the form of voting shares. Workers should have strong representation on boards of directors. Public capital should be available to encourage formation of producer and consumer co-ops on a significant scale. One or two Crown corporations – starting perhaps with the CNR – might be turned over to the employees over a period of years to operate as democratically as possible, subject of course to the final responsibility of Parliament. Federal government departments should be at the fore-front of experiments to break down the tyranny of bureaucracy by involving workers at all levels in the design of their jobs, management decision-making and policy planning.

The object of democracy is to ensure that power is exercised in the public interest, rather than for private advantage, and it seems inevitable and desirable that the principle will be extended to govern not only political power, but also economic power. Indeed, the rights of private owners of property have already been curtailed by numerous laws, and the process will continue until, at some stage in the distant future, private control will have given away entirely to various forms of public control.

PART THREE: SUPRANATIONALISM

8

The International Society

When the first European settlers arrived in North America, there were already scores of well-established nations spread across the continent. There were probably as many as a million native people organized in tribes and federations, with their distinctive cultures, economies, and forms of government. To them, society must have seemed stable and the world settled on its course. But with the arrival of the Europeans, with their new ideas and technology, there soon began a process of political change and social upheaval that still continues. The native nations were gradually brought under the rule of the European colonists, by treaty, conquest, or simple assimilation. The colonists fought among each other to establish empires, and then joined forces to seek independence from imperial control. The American colonies fought their War of Independence just 200 years ago, and the new country began the expansion and consolidation that is not yet finished. It is only in recent years that Hawaii and Alaska have become full States of the Union, and it was only in 1976 that the United States pushed its borders 200 miles out to sea. Here in Canada, four colonies united only a little over a century ago and the process of Confederation is continuing. Newfoundland elected to enter in 1949. Canada is still striving to establish its sovereignty over huge areas of the Arctic and over coastal waters.

Thus in 400 years the political organization of this continent has undergone a series of changes in which the persistent trend has been to merge small states into ever larger states. The number of self-governing nations has been reduced from scores to just two – Canada and the United States. The process of consolidation has owed less to the design of empire builders than the accident of new technologies that have altered patterns of trade, means of communication, and the necessities of military defence. At every stage there has been resistance by those who wanted to conserve the existing nation or state, with its distinctive culture and society; and even the leaders of change have often been reluctant revolutionaries driven by circumstances to break through the existing borders to build new, larger, and more viable states. The status quo has seldom been an option. The fathers of the American revolution were hesitant rebels against British rule. The concept of the Canadian federation grew out of the deadlock and frustration in the United Province of Ontario and Quebec. It was only when John A. Macdonald and others became convinced that the United Province was not a satisfactory state that they turned to the idea of joining with other colonies to form a larger country. They, too, encountered stubborn resistance among local patriots. The decision in favour of Confederation carried only narrowly in the Maritimes. French Canadians were far from enthusiastic. In the West, the Métis took up arms against the encroaching Canadians. But always the compelling need to create larger and larger units for trade and defence overwhelmed those who wanted to preserve local control and the established society.

A similar trend of consolidation of small nations into larger and larger states can be observed in Europe. Germany and Italy and many of the other great national states that we now regard as part of the natural order because they have existed through our lifetime were unified only in the last century. Now we see these great European states, which seemed so prominent and powerful and such implacable enemies less than forty years ago, joining in a new superstate – the European Economic Community. They are seeking political as well as economic integration, and even Britain, with its world view based on memories of empire, attachment to the Commonwealth, and special relationships across the Atlantic, has been driven by economics to become a member of the union and to surrender part of that national sovereignty it has held so dear.

If the forces driving toward integration can lead historic enemies in Europe to overcome the differences of race and language, forget their hatreds, and seek political unity, we have to ask if in North America we are really stabilized in two great states. Have the forces of consolidation at last run out of steam? The answer is no. The forces of consolidation are stronger than ever, and they have already brought about substantial integration, not only of Canada with the United States, but of all the highly developed industrial democracies. We Canadians are in fact already part of a new society that transcends political borders.

We share a way of life and a set of values with people in the United States and Western Europe and other countries at a similar stage of development. We read the same books and magazines, watch the same television and movies, listen to the same modern music and absorb the same messages from the lyrics, live in similar houses in similar suburbs or in almost identical apartment buildings, drive the same cars and obey the same traffic signs, eat the same foods and drink the same drinks, pop the same tranquillizers, work for the same corporations, enjoy the same sports, direct dial across oceans or travel casually at jet speed across mountain barriers that historically divided nations, to stay in identical hotels. We are also part of a supranational economy in which capital, managers, technicians, and scientific know-how move easily across borders organizing economic activity on a world scale. Our politics tend to become more and more like the politics of other countries at a similar stage of development because we share the same goals of peace, prosperity, and freedom, and the same problems of inflation, unemployment, pollution, and relations with the Communist countries and the Third World of developing states. The growth of the supranational system imposes severe limits on the freedom of our national governments to pursue independent policies. Defence systems, for example, have become so complex and costly that it is impractical for any country except a super power to pretend to defend itself. So our defence policies are integrated through the North Atlantic Treaty Organization, and we have only limited sovereignty in deciding how much of our national income to spend on defence, how many men and women to maintain in uniform, and in what formations to organize them, and with what weapons to equip them. We are required to consult our allies about all these matters. If we try to be too independent, they make their displeasure known, and we soon find it is to our advantage to meet them at least halfway. Similarly, national governments have to keep their economic policies roughly in step with those of their neighbours and competitors. A country that gets too far out of line on tax or monetary or tariff policies will find capital and knowledge and even skilled labour moving to more hospitable countries within the system. Our economic problems and the solutions to them have to be seen in an international context because we recognize the extent to which our business affairs are integrated with those of other countries. This interdependence explains the proliferation of international organizations that seek to co-ordinate national economic policies: the Organization for Economic Co-operation and Development, the International Monetary Fund, the Central Bankers, the International Energy Agency of eighteen industrialized countries, and many others.

Although we may worry about cultural identity, the inescapable fact is that television signals know no borders, that movies create the same illusions of reality for us all, and it is inconceivable that democratic governments could interfere seriously with the mass distribution of books within the supranational system. So, although the developed democracies maintain the forms and institutions of independent national states, their borders no longer define distinctive national cultures or self-regulating national economies or national political systems capable of defending themselves.

The growth of the supranational system has made possible a great enrichment in the lives of most Canadians. The flow of people, capital, technology, and trade has stimulated our economy to expand at an extraordinary rate. The real value of our production more than tripled in the quarter century from 1950 to 1975. The purchasing power of the average income, after tax, has more than doubled since the Second World War. Although it is fashionable to discount the social value of economic growth, the truth remains that rising incomes mean increasing freedom for individual Canadians to live their lives as they think best – free to seek higher education, choose a career, pursue a sport or hobby, develop a talent, travel, indulge a fancy for food or drink or entertainment. Free, in short, to make all the choices that are not open to poorer people. We have also been enjoying an extraordinary cultural boom, both in the volume of art and entertainment being produced in Canada and in the greater access we have to the cultures of other countries through films, television, and cheap travel.

We take such marvels for granted but they are in large part the product of the new organization of economic and cultural activities that has developed over the past thirty-five years, mainly in the countries around the Atlantic. Many Canadians are now persuaded, however, that the price for this enrichment of our lives has been too high. They argue we have borrowed too much foreign capital, sold our industry and resources, betrayed our cultural heritage. We are urged to resist the forces that are leading us toward the construction of the supranational society and to raise barriers against the world so that we can concentrate on building a distinctive national economy and culture to ensure national independence. Nationalists have already had remarkable success in changing public attitudes and political policies. The heresy of the sixties when nationalists were on the fringes of power has become the dogma of the seventies in many of the centres that mould and manipulate public opinion: the mass media, schools and universities, the political parties. It is not surprising, therefore, that polls report that the majority of Canadians are opposed to further foreign investment and prepared even to suffer a reduction in their standard of living to "buy back" Canadian industry.

The federal and provincial governments have naturally responded to the changes in public opinion and have introduced a number of protectionist measures. Proposals for new foreign investment are now screened to see if they will meet the test of significant benefit to Canada. Foreign-owned corporations are required to appoint Canadian directors. The Canadian Radio and Television Commission has imposed Canadian-content rules on radio and TV broadcasting and has tried to find a way to reduce the amount of U.S. programming coming across the border by cable and by air. *Time* magazine has been forced to discontinue its Canadian edition to make advertising available for Canadian periodicals. In some provinces there are restrictions on ownership of land by foreigners, policies to support Canadian book-publishers, and pressure to reduce the number of foreign professors in universities. Taken together with earlier actions that forbade the foreign control of banks and other financial institutions, and of newspapers, magazines, and broadcasting companies, these policies represent a significant shift toward economic and cultural nationalism. Foreign policy also has been adjusted toward a more nationalist stance, and the official strategy is now what is known as the Third Option, which is to reduce Canadian dependence on the United States by strengthening ties with other countries.

Much of what has been done makes good sense. While national states are of declining importance in the supranational system, we certainly continue to have national interests to protect, at least in the short-term. The danger is that nationalist policies pursued too far will divert us from learning to live and compete in the new supranational economy in which our future must lie.

We can be sure also that the great majority of Canadian nationalists are responsible patriots, far removed from the fanatics who have laid waste so many other countries in the name of nationalism. The danger is that nationalism has a history of getting out of control. To encourage Canadians to be more interested in their history, more receptive to their artists, more concerned with national problems, is commendable. To encourage Canadians to fear or hate their neighbours, even to feel superior to Americans, is detestable. It is regrettably easy to find examples of this sort of propaganda in current fiction, journalism, and politics.

George Woodcock, the writer and anarchist who has experienced European politics at first-hand, wrote an article in *The Canadian Forum* in 1973 welcoming what he called liberation from the American chaos, but adding: "I feel an uneasiness amounting to alarm when I observe nationalism emerging out of this situation. I am told – indeed I have been told by some of the editors of *The Canadian Forum* – that nationalism in Canada is not the same as classic European nationalism, that it is a milder

166

and less dangerous virus. I am not convinced, although I am ready to make distinctions among those in Canada who call themselves nationalists." Among those who responded to Woodcock was Ed Broadbent, a politician and political scientist, and now leader of the New Democratic Party. While affirming his desire to regain for Canada freedom for what he called the political, economic, and cultural domination of the United States, he acknowledged that in history nationalism has normally been "an exclusive, intolerant, xenophobic movement. As a force, it has tended to swamp with its negative qualities the positive aspects of both liberalism and socialism with which it has so frequently simultaneously emerged . . . . In short, those of us on the Left who want both an independent and a socialist Canada should take care to avoid promoting within our country attitudes and institutions that would vitiate our liberation objective." It is not clear to what expressions of nationalism Woodcock was objecting, or what degree of nationalism Broadbent finds acceptable. But it is certainly true that nationalist rhetoric has become more shrill in recent years. Otherwise sensible Canadians have been conditioned to think of themselves as oppressed and exploited subjects of the U.S. empire, despite the obvious fact that they are among the freest and wealthiest people the world has ever known.

We can hope that the limits of nationalism, and of its offspring, anti-Americanism, have now been reached in Canada. But observing how rapidly opinion has shifted in the past dozen years, who can be sure what will happen unless we pay attention to the real world in which we live? The purpose of this chapter is to examine that real world and its economic impact on Canada. The following chapter will examine the cultural impact. The argument to be made is that in this western world of international dependency, multinational organization of business, and supranational culture, nationalism is an idea whose time has passed. We are in the age of interdependence and not of independence.

FOREIGN INVESTMENT

Foreign business investment is the best-known example of Canada's involvement in the supranational economic system, and there have been two major studies of this phenomenon. Walter Gordon, correctly described by his biographer as the "gentle patriot," established the Task Force on the Structures of Canadian Industry, when he was a minister in the Pearson government. He appointed as chairman Mel Watkins, an economist who later became leader of the arch-nationalist Waffle faction of the NDP. The report of the task force in 1968 became known as the Watkins report. The Trudeau Cabinet subsequently commissioned a more detailed study by the Working Group on Foreign Direct Investment in Canada. It was directed by Herbert Gray, then a minister without portfolio, and its 1972 report was known as the Gray report. Both studies concluded that the level of foreign investment and control in Canada was so high as to be a cause for general concern and to create specific problems. But both reports also said plainly that foreign investment has brought benefits to Canada and will remain important for Canadian development for years to come. Neither report proposed cutting off the flow of investment into Canada, let alone expelling foreign corporations already here. Neither was antagonistic in tone toward U.S. investment. The Watkins report said:

> Direct investment, as a package of product, management, capital and market access, brings with it large potential economic benefits for the host country; certainly these benefits are larger than are imagined by those who conceive of foreign investment as being simply a capital flow. Undoubtedly, a host country which restricted foreign investment, and did nothing else, would risk creating economic stagnation and turning the country into a technological backwater. Furthermore, with economic benefit can come national political benefit. A rich and growing country is more capable of pursuing independent policies at home and abroad than one that is poor and stagnant. It is clear that both economic benefits and economic costs can inhere in foreign investment. The major economic benefit is the contribution to economic growth. The major economic cost is the possible impediments to the creation of a more independent national economy.

The Gray report put it in this way: "If foreign direct investment merely created problems it would be a simple matter to deal with it: all foreign investments could simply be blocked. But in many cases foreign investment is a complex mix of costs and benefits both of which are extremely difficult to quantify in economic terms, to say nothing of social, cultural and political terms – for the nation as a whole." Both studies recognized explicitly the continuing importance of foreign investment and its accompanying assets, and both said that the thrust of government policy should be to reduce the costs and increase the benefits. Neither report suggested that Canada could opt out of the new economic system in which trade and commerce are increasingly organized on a supranational basis.

It is sometimes said that we could have obtained all or most of the benefits of economic growth without allowing foreigners to take over Canadian companies or to own our natural resources. We could, it is said, have borrowed capital and paid it back out of profits, instead of allowing foreigners to own corporations in Canada and take the profit forever. We could have rented the right to use foreign technology. No doubt we could have been a lot wiser than we have been. But the important thing to bear in mind is that it was Canadians and not foreigners who wanted things this way. Foreign manufacturers would have been glad to invest their capital at home in bigger factories and sell us their products in the normal way. But we wanted to develop manufacturing industry in Canada; so we raised tariff barriers to keep out those foreign goods. As a result, foreigners with goods and services to sell had to come into Canada and set up business.

Until fairly recently most Canadians could see nothing wrong with that. We got the capital, the technology, the new products, the jobs, exports, and taxes. But as the Watkins and Gray reports have shown, we also got some real disadvantages. Principally, we got what has come to be called a "branch-plant economy" made up of truncated companies. The foreign subsidiary established in Canada tends naturally to be merely a branch of the parent company in the United States, Europe, or Japan. It produces the same product in the same way and distributes and markets it in the same way, making only minor changes to take account of Canadian conditions. The research and development is done at the head office. The top managers are trained at the head office. The head office decides where and when the Canadian subsidiary can export its products.

What's more, there tend to be too many foreign subsidiaries

competing for shares of the small Canadian market. The U.S. market is large enough to absorb the output of, say, ten corporations producing similar products on an efficient scale. But if all ten U.S. corporations set up subsidiaries to produce in Canada, none of them will have enough of the market to operate efficiently. A 1960 study, for example, found the Canadian market could have been served by one large plant producing electric ranges, but there were in fact twenty-three plants.

There is the problem also that, as the Gray report put it, "The investment decisions of foreign-controlled corporations tend to reflect the laws and industrial priorities of foreign governments and economies which in turn influence Canadian industrial priorities." Or if the subsidiary is part of a multinational corporation operating in many countries, it may be subject to rule from head office that effectively transcends the laws of all countries.

These, then, are some of the advantages and disadvantages attaching to foreign investment and control. Basically, we gain prosperity and economic growth at the cost of a certain loss of efficiency, initiative, and autonomy. It is surely clear then that foreign investment is not a simple issue. To repeat, both the Watkins and the Gray reports emphasized that it is a complicated phenomenon, and both suggested a mix of policies – some of which have since been implemented – designed to maintain maximum advantage at minimum cost. The Watkins report said: "Canadian policies must be directed towards increasing the benefits and decreasing the costs of foreign direct investment." The Gray report echoed: "Since foreign direct investment will likely continue to be an important factor in Canada for years to come, Canadians must explore alternative means of reducing the cost of foreign investment and increasing to the greatest extent possible the benefits which it can bring to the nation over the long term."

Let us now look more closely at the complexity of the problems.

Resources
Foreign corporations have invested heavily in Canadian

resources, usually to secure a supply of raw materials they can ship to processing plants and factories in the United States and in other countries. But Canada has often been glad to get development capital from foreign corporations that also provided an assured market for raw materials. As the Gray report explained, when weighing the pros and cons of the situation:

> An independent developer of natural resources is in a risky position. The capital investment is generally substantial. The potential purchasers of raw materials are few. Consequently the resource developer is in the position of having to commit large sums of money with the return being dependent on his skills as a bargainer, rather than on open-market sales to a large number of independent purchasers. While this is not valid for every resource commodity, there are numerous segments of the industry in which this confrontation has led to vertical integration in the interests of both suppliers and purchasers. Furthermore as pointed out above, without a secure market, financing for such projects is often unavailable.

It is hardly fair, therefore, to picture foreign investors as rapacious exploiters of virgin Canada leaving us with empty oil wells and worked out mines. But there remains the question of whether the resources are being sold off at such a rate as to endanger the future.

The federal and provincial ministers reponsible for resources published in 1974 a report titled "Towards a Mineral Policy for Canada" in which they assessed resources against needs and said: "Even if all exploration and technological progress stopped immediately, Canada's current mineral reserves would be adequate to meet domestic needs far into the future for the major commodities Canada now produces." Pointing out that most exploration and development was undertaken to meet foreign demand rather that the needs of the limited Canadian market, the ministers said: "In relation to domestic needs our present reserves are very large. . . . This is particularly true for potash, asbestos and iron, each of which shows reserves of at least one hundred times the total domestic need for the year 2000. Reserves for other important minerals listed [copper, lead, nickel, zinc] are at least five times our needs for the year 2000. Thus, if exports were discouraged, little incentive to continue exploration would exist for many years." In other words, if foreign corporations were banned from exporting resource materials Canadians would have enough to last well into the next century, and there would be no point in prospecting for new discoveries and developing new mines. But the ministers said that if the exploration does continue there are "excellent" chances of developing major new reserves of copper, iron, lead, molybdenum, nickel, potash, sulphur, and zinc.

Oil and gas are a different matter. Although the world's first oil company was formed in Ontario in 1850 to produce oil near Sarnia, the industry grew much faster in the United States, where larger discoveries were made. In 1914, oil was found in British Columbia, and in 1920 the first Arctic oil was found by Imperial Oil, a subsidiary of the U.S. giant, Standard Oil, at Norman Wells, close to the Arctic Circle. But demand in Canada grew much faster than the domestic supply, and during the Second World War, Canada was largely dependent on supplies from the United States – a point worth bearing in mind. By 1946 daily demand was 221,000 barrels and imports made up 200,000 barrels of this. Imperial Oil meanwhile had sunk some $30 million in drilling 133 dry holes. Finally, in 1946, Imperial drilled the famous Leduc #1 near Edmonton and ushered in the great oil-boom that transformed Alberta from a rather poor and backward province into one of the richest and most ambitious. But the major market for Alberta and later Saskatchewan oil and natural gas was in the United States.

It was the policy of successive Canadian governments to import foreign oil, mostly from Venezuela, for use in Quebec and the Atlantic region, while Ontario and the west were reserved as a market for Canadian oil. A trans-Canada pipeline was built, by American entrepreneurs, to move natural gas from the west to the east, but the oil line stopped in Ontario. Why? Because foreign oil was substantially cheaper in Montreal than Canadian oil. For years Canada made a profit on international oil-trade by selling high-cost western oil to the United States while importing low-priced foreign oil in the east. The United States was prepared to pay the higher Canadian price because it was a secure supply – that is, it reduced U.S. dependence on supplies from less reliable sources in Latin America and the Middle East. Washington was troubled, in fact, because Canada, having no transcontinental pipeline, was largely dependent on foreign oil, and on the United States in a world emergency. The concern was justified because in 1956 and again in 1967, when crises in the Middle East disrupted the world oil-trade and the great Montreal refinery complex ran short of supplies, Canada appealed to the United States for help, and supplies were pumped up to Montreal from south of the border. In return, Canada increased supplies to the western United States. The fact remained, however, that in the pinch Canada was at least as dependent on oil from the United States as the United States was on Canada. The U.S. government frequently urged Canada to secure its own supply by building a trans-Canada pipeline so that Montreal would not be dependent in a crisis on supplies from the United States. But it was not until foreign oil suddenly skyrocketed in price in the 1973-74 energy crisis that the Canadian government decided to complete the trans-Canada line, linking Alberta to Montreal.

Canadian policy for many years, therefore, was to sell as much western oil as possible to the United States. In this, federal governments were encouraged by Alberta governments and by spokesmen for opposition parties who complained that the United States was unfairly restricting imports of Canadian oil. As late as 1969, Prime Minister Trudeau went to Washington to meet President Richard Nixon and urge, among other things, that the United States should buy more Canadian oil. The two national leaders, in their communique, affirmed "agreement with respect to our community of interests in the expansion of energy movements across our border," and Trudeau spoke at a press conference about "a continental energy policy of sorts."

Exports of oil and gas were, of course, subject to licensing by the National Energy Board, a federal agency charged with ensuring that adequate supplies remain for Canadian use. Therefore, early in the 1970s, when it began to become apparent that Canada had only enough conventional oil left to meet demand for ten or fifteen years, the question was asked: How did this happen? Why had we been pumping oil into the United States when there would not be enough to serve Canadian needs?

173

It was obvious that the National Energy Board and the Alberta agencies had been too optimistic about discoveries of new resources. Foreign corporations, controlling about 90 per cent of the industry, had misled the board with inflated estimates of oil and gas reserves in order to be able to export to parent companies in the United States. But it was not only the companies that believed there were huge reserves waiting to be discovered and developed in Canada. The federal government published in 1973 a study entitled *An Energy Policy for Canada* in which it said: "It is believed that most of Canada's ultimate potential oil remains to be discovered." The report explained that relatively little exploration had been undertaken in the so-called frontier areas, in the Arctic, and off the coast, and continued: "The Geological Survey of Canada, however, has begun a program of regular estimates of Canada's oil and gas potential. These estimates are based on the geological analysis of all the sedimentary basins in Canada and make use of comparisons with other petroleum-producing basins throughout the world." In 1969 the Canadian Petroleum Association, which is dominated by foreign-owned companies, estimated Canada's oil potential at 120.9 billion barrels and gas at 724.8 trillion cubic feet. Three years later, in 1972, the government's own geological survey upped the estimates to 134.4 billion barrels of oil and 906.2 trillion cubic feet of gas. In other words, the government's own experts were more optimistic than the foreign-owned companies.

Since then estimates have been coming down rapidly because the record of discoveries has been disappointing. Oil and gas are not being found where the experts thought they would be. The Energy Board and the federal Department of Energy, Mines, and Resources have become far more sophisticated and cautious in estimating how much oil can be extracted from crude reserves and about the chances of discovering new oil at acceptable prices. Even so the export policy of the past certainly has been unwise, counting too much on resources expected to be discovered. If we have to find scapegoats for what may prove to have been a shortsighted or even disastrous energy policy, Liberal and Conservative governments in Ottawa, Social Credit and Conservative governments in Alberta, and even C.C.F.-N.D.P. governments

174

in Saskatchewan carry some responsibility with the oil companies.

Nobody can say what would have happened in Canada if foreign investment in energy resources had been excluded or accepted at a much lower rate. But the truth probably is that there was never a realistic political choice. No government, however farsighted, in Ottawa or in Edmonton, could have told Albertans that they were not going to be allowed to develop their great natural wealth as fast as capital investment, technology, and markets would allow. It would have been equivalent to telling British Columbians not to cut their trees or catch their fish, or telling people in Ontario not to develop secondary industry. Growth was the goal in Canada during the fifties and sixties, and Alberta and the west were anxious to develop natural resources. Canadian public policy offered incentives to growth; and as the White Paper on energy policy pointed out, in the oil and gas sector, "Foreign firms were in a position to take advantage of these opportunities and incentives."

The priority in the seventies and the eighties will be to develop new energy sources. Huge amounts of capital will be needed to explore in the Arctic and under the seas, build pipelines, and mine oil from the western tar sands, one of the world's great reserves, but expensive even by modern standards. When the federal government published (in 1976) its conclusions about energy policy under the title *An Energy Strategy for Canada – Policies for Self-Reliance*, it said there was a need to invest as much as $180 billion in energy development over the next fifteen years. Although committed to securing higher levels of Canadian ownership and participation in the energy industry in future, the government also admitted that "Canada must continue to rely substantially on foreign capital in the future." The Economic Council of Canada had come to a similar conclusion earlier. After assessing all Canada's development and capital needs in the light of the energy shortage, it concluded: "Canada faces formidable capital requirements over the coming years. To finance these investments would require that resources be drawn from outside Canada to supplement domestic savings."

In short, whatever may be thought about foreign investment in resource industries in the past, there is probably going to be a great deal more of it in the future. The problem will be to ensure there is adequate regulation of foreign corporations by Canadian governments.

Research and Development
Another cause for concern about the level of foreign ownership in Canada is that it inhibits research and development which are the keys to modern industrial growth. As the Senate Committee on Science Policy noted, ownership of land was the source of wealth and power in feudal times; with the Industrial Revolution, power passed to those who controlled the mines and factories; and in modern times, when production of wealth depends on the application of scientific knowledge to industry, power lies with those who possess technology. It can be argued that a national economy that lacks the capacity to create new products and solve production problems through scientific research and development will be, in effect, the colony of more advanced countries. In Canada it is feared that foreign-owned subsidiary corporations will simply import technology from their parent companies abroad instead of doing research and development here. Canada will thus never develop the research and development capacity to be a modern and independent country, and Canadians who want to be at the forefront of industrial development will have to go abroad to make careers in the central laboratories of giant corporations. The Watkins report described the issue in this way: "Direct investment brings a variety of techniques to the recipient country, including management skills, labour training, the results of research and development, production know-how and other information. The concern expressed in Canada in these respects is that the ease of access to such techniques from the parent may cause the subsidiary to neglect the development of skills within Canada."

Unfortunately there is now no doubt that Canada is backward in technological development. The Organization for Economic Co-operation and Development devised four scales for measuring technological innovation in ten advanced countries in the 1960s, and Canada came tenth. The Senate Committee on Science Policy pointed out that Canada spends a smaller proportion of gross national product on research and development than most similar countries, and there are other studies that confirm Canada's weak effort. But the causes are not simply the result of foreign ownership. The Watkins report compared the research effort of Canadian-controlled and foreign-controlled corporations in Canada. Making allowance for the fact that foreign ownership is concentrated in new, high-technology industries that might be expected to do more research than older industries in which Canadian control is strong, it nevertheless concluded: "The evidence, then, is that foreign subsidiaries perform as well as or better than Canadian-owned firms in terms of R and D." The Senate Committee accepted much the same conclusion: "All the available evidence shows that at least until recently foreign-owned subsidiaries spent proportionately as much on R and D as similar Canadian companies, if not more." The senators also quoted an OECD study that compared the science policy of the hundred most important firms in Canada and concluded: "Firms under non-Canadian control quite definitely spend more on R and D than the Canadian firms." The Senate report suggested, however, that the situation might be changing as Canadian-controlled firms spent more on research while foreign-controlled firms spent less. The Gray report also noted such a trend but was cautious: "It would appear that the R and D efforts of Canadian-controlled firms has recently compared more favourably with the foreign-controlled sector than previously. . . . It is too soon however to be sure exactly why these changes have occurred and whether they indicate anything more than temporary cyclical changes."

The Gray report identified three reasons why Canada has a poor performance in innovation. First, companies with access to large potential markets such as in the United States are more likely to invest in research and development than companies competing in a small market such as Canada. Second, multinational firms operating in several countries prefer to concentrate their research at headquarters, usually in the United States, and foreign subsidiaries in Canada and elsewhere are not given the opportunity to do as much research. Third – and this point was emphasized also in the Senate report – Canada has tended to concentrate on basic and applied research in government and university laboratories, whereas other countries have encouraged commercial development by industry. Having mentioned foreign ownership as one cause of the poor performance, the Gray report cautioned: "This does not necessarily mean that in the absence of foreign control in these industries, more R and D expenditures would take place, although recent trends over the past decade of a few Canadian-controlled companies in advanced technological industries, such as Northern Electric, suggest that this is a possibility."

The Senate Committee found that there is a need for nothing less than a transformation of Canadian ideas and attitudes. "We are deeply convinced that it is in the country's best long-term interest to make a substantial shift in Canadian growth objectives and strategies as quickly as possible." The senators borrowed from Alvin Toffler's best-selling book, *Future Shock,* the idea of an anticipatory democracy in which all segments of the population join in planning the future, and prescribed:

> Business management of secondary manufacturing and resource-based industries will have to forget the growth patterns of the past and learn how to live and expand with the delicate innovative process, which is a perpetual new beginning. Canadian workers, who have always been quite mobile, will have to adapt even more quickly to rapid technological change. Students, universities, and the scientific and engineering community will have to change motivation and agree to participate more actively than in the past in the economic progress of their country. Above all, public authorities and particularly the Canadian government will not only have to support the new industrial and technological strategy but also plan forward to maximize benefits and minimize the negative effects of innovation. What we need in fact is a new national policy, a technological strategy that combines science policy and industrial policy into a new innovative synthesis.

With less imagination but perhaps more realism, the Gray report concluded:

> Canada is very heavily dependent on foreign technology, much of which enters in the form of direct investment. Some reasons have been adduced for suggesting it is in the Canadian interest to reduce the degree of Canada's dependence on exter-

nal sources. However, even if Canada increases its technological output very substantially, it will still remain very heavily dependent on external technology. For the great range of Canadian needs, technology will have to enter either in the form of finished products, direct investment or on licence.

The real problem, therefore, is to ensure that Canada gets the greatest benefit at the lowest cost from foreign technology, suggested the Gray report.

In summary, Canada is weak in the vital area of research and development. One of several reasons for the weakness is the high level of foreign ownership, although this also brings benefits in the form of cheap technology from abroad. There is no solution to be found in attacking foreign corporations on whom we shall continue to rely for much of our technology in the future. Instead, we must seek to develop better science policies in Canada. The federal government did establish in 1971 a special Ministry of State for Science and Technology, which was to be a new sort of federal ministry committed to research, consultation with other departments, and the formulation of science policy, rather than the administration of new programs. But when the Science Council of Canada, yet another federal body advising on science policy, undertook a study of the new ministry, its two researchers, Peter Aucoin and Richard French, found that little had been accomplished. They said the Ministry-of-State concept was based on the idea that "knowledge is power" and that rational planning based on research, consultation, analysis, and policy formulation would replace the power brokerage and horsetrading in Cabinet decision-making about science policies. Lacking the political power that derives from control of major spending programs in the old-line departments, however, the Minister of Science had little to trade in the Cabinet and was outside the closed circle of decision-makers. The failure of science policy and the weakness of research and development in Canada are therefore a failure of government policy.

Rule of (Foreign) Law
Another problem arising from foreign investment, which generates newspaper headlines and therefore attracts a great deal of public interest, is the attempt by foreign governments to impose

their law or policy upon corporations in Canada. The United States, for example, for many years forbade corporations under its jurisdiction to trade with "enemy" countries such as Cuba, and this law applied to subsidiaries in Canada of U.S. corporations. So, while the Canadian government encouraged trade with Cuba, U.S.-owned corporations in Canada were forbidden by U.S. law to export their goods to Cuba. In other words, the U.S. government was trying to make its law extend beyond its own territory into Canadian territory.

There are other examples of this intrusion, which is known technically as "extraterritoriality." The United States has a tough anti-monopolies law to try to maintain competition between corporations. The Department of Justice in Washington, D.C., and the federal courts can forbid mergers or even order the breakup of big companies. The major companies affected by U.S. law sometimes have subsidiaries in Canada, and U.S. law is made to apply to them – that is, they are forbidden to merge, or they are ordered to dissolve although there may be no such requirement in Canadian law or policy. American-owned corporations in Canada have been known also to ask the U.S. government to put diplomatic pressure on the Canadian government to change a law or policy to which the corporation objects.

There are other less obvious and more technical ways in which foreign law and policy intrude into Canada through foreign-owned corporations, and they are all an affront to Canadian sovereignty which journalists and politicians find easy to exploit. When it is discovered, for example, that a foreign-owned company is hesitating to accept an export order because it might run foul of U.S. law, there is great indignation in Canada. It is seen as a simple case of the United States infringing on Canadian sovereignty, which makes for exciting headlines, angry editorials, and outraged speeches in the House of Commons. The Watkins report said flatly: "The most apparent political cost to the host country of foreign ownership results from extraterritoriality." The Gray report declared: "As a matter of principle, Canada has a right to exercise full control over activities that occur within its borders – and should assert this right. The direction of behaviour within Canada by foreign governments offends this principle." Both studies, it will be noted, were talking about intangibles.

Watkins emphasized the political cost of loss of sovereignty rather than measurable economic loss, and Gray discussed the issue in terms of principle. There are few if any documented cases in which Canada has actually suffered an economic loss as a result of the intervention of foreign law. This is not to say that no loss has ever occurred. It may be that foreign-owned companies in Canada have not sought export business that they could and would have got had they not been deterred by law in their home country. American-owned companies, for example, were not likely to be active in trying to sell to Cuba when their own home government forbade them to do so. But if and when potential orders were passed up in this passive way, no record was kept and there is no way of totting up the total. On the other hand, when cases *have* come to light of foreign companies hesitating to fill export orders they have usually been speedily corrected. American-owned mills in Canada once refused to ship flour to Cuba, but Canadian mills eagerly took the order. On other occasions, the Canadian government has made it plain to the foreign subsidiary that it is expected to ignore the U.S. law and to act in conformity with Canadian policy. In those cases the U.S. government has usually turned a blind eye. In fact the U.S. law that forbade trading with enemies such as Cuba and China seemed over the years to be increasingly regarded as an anachronism dating from the days of the Cold War, and there was no great zeal in Washington to enforce it.

The Gray report pointed out that the United States is not unusual among countries in seeking to extend its law and policy to the operation of subsidiaries in other countries. All countries do it to some extent. If they did not, they would simply be inviting their corporations to evade law by establishing foreign subsidiaries that could do as they pleased. For example, a Canadian corporation forbidden by Ottawa to ship war materials to the Middle East could set up a subsidiary in a third country and export through it, thus evading Canadian policy.

What makes the U.S. situation unusual is that the United States has so many foreign subsidiaries and that they form such a large part of the Canadian economy. The problem is not really one of principle, but of scale. It is ironic also that some Canadians who object loudly when U.S. law intrudes into Canada call on the Canadian government to behave in exactly the same way. Convinced that Canadian-owned companies are exploiting the workers in Latin America or in Africa, they demand that the Canadian government do something to correct the injustice. They want Ottawa to apply Canadian policy to the operation of the Canadian companies in other countries. That's an example of extraterritoriality and the truth may be that to a certain extent it is unavoidable when business transcends national borders.

Multinationals

A writer in the British left-wing journal *The New Statesman* suggested ironically that socialists must always have a demon to blame for events. At one time it was "the brewers" who corrupted the workers. Then it was the "merchants of death" who promoted war and spilt the blood of the workers. Now it is multinational corporations that are said to exploit not only workers but whole nations. But it is not only socialists who think this way. Multinational corporations have become a popular villain on which to blame all our economic and political problems. The very word "multinational" has become a dirty word. These giant corporations are accused of depleting natural resources, cheating workers and consumers, corrupting politicians, and evading the just laws and policies of national governments – all in the pursuit of immense private profits. There is no doubt multinational corporations do commit some of these crimes some of the time. Recent Senate investigations in the United States have exposed the extent to which these corporations have bribed politicians and others in foreign countries and contributed to the defeat of governments that seemed likely to curb their business operations. But national corporations have also been found guilty of corruption and interference in political affairs, particularly in the earlier days of robber tycoons. And even governments have been known to misbehave from time to time.

There seems no reason to believe that multinational corporations are any more or less moral than other human institutions. Against their vices must be set their virtues. They bring together on a huge scale capital, labour, technology, management, and markets, and their success in producing goods that people wish to buy is shown by their rapid growth. *Multinational Corporations*

182

in World Development, a United Nations study published in 1973, counted some 7,300 corporations with affiliates in at least one foreign country, but focused attention on a few hundred of the largest:

A central characteristic of multinational corporations is the predominance of large-sized firms. Typically, the amount of annual sales runs into the hundreds of millions of dollars. Each of the largest four multinational corporations has a sales volume in excess of $10 billion, and more than 200 multinational corporations have surpassed the $1 billion level. Indeed, for most practical purposes, those with less than $100 million in sales can safely be ignored. The very size of these corporations as compared with other economic entities, including the economies of many nations, suggests an important source of power. Moreover, there are strong indications that the multinational corporations have grown dramatically, especially during the last decade.

The UN study identified nearly 200 corporations with affiliates in twenty or more countries. Drawing on the considerable literature about multinational corporations that has appeared in recent years, the Gray report noted:
- Sixty-two of the top 100 U.S. corporations have production facilities in at least six foreign countries.
- Seventy-one of the top 126 industrial corporations have one-third of their employees abroad.
- About eighty per cent of all U.S. foreign direct investment is accounted for by some 200 firms (for example, General Motors, Chrysler, Ford, Singer, Exxon, ITT).
- There are about 100 major multinational corporations based outside the United States (for example, Nestlé, Shell, Lever Bros.).
- U.S. subsidiaries in foreign countries have sales of over $200 billion a year.
- Foreign subsidiaries in the United States have sales of about $100 billion a year.
- Total annual value of goods and services produced in the non-Communist world has been estimated at $2,350 billion. Of this, 19 per cent is controlled by foreign-controlled subsidiaries.

183

The Gray study concluded that on the basis of very conservative estimates, multinational corporations will continue to grow and become increasingly powerful institutions; and it noted, although with some scepticism, the forecast of one observer that by 1990 they may account for half the gross national product of the entire free world: "The world's economy will be dominated by three hundred or four hundred MNEs (multinational enterprises). It will not be unusual for an MNE to have one million employees." The Economic Council of Canada, in its report, *Looking Outward*, published in 1975, confirmed the growing importance of multinational corporations in world trade and pointed out that corporations based in Europe and Japan are expanding rapidly to compete with the u.s. giants. "Concern with this problem has been widespread in recent years, with various proposals being put forward for international regulation of multinational firms, as well as for more traditional national control of competition," said the Council. "Whatever comes of these ideas, there seems little doubt that some type of multinational enterprise will exist through the coming decades as a major catalyst of industrial development around the world." Although foreign investment used to be concentrated in underdeveloped colonial countries to supply raw materials to advanced industrial countries, multinational corporations now operate mostly in developed countries where they manufacture and market their specialized, high-technology products. The Gray report said that in 1969 42 per cent of u.s. foreign investment was in manufacturing and 36 per cent in natural resources.

Canada is both host and home for multinational corporations. That is, most of the big u.s., European, and Japanese corporations have subsidiaries here, and some Canadian-owned corporations have subsidiaries abroad. Canadians are substantial investors abroad, and the Watkins report pointed out that on a *per capita* basis, Canadians own more of the United States than u.s. citizens own of Canada. But this is misleading for a couple of reasons. Canadian investment in the United States is not concentrated to the same degree as u.s. investment in Canada and does not give control of corporations and industries on the same scale. Second, about 40 per cent of the capital going out of Canada to be invested abroad is owned by foreign-controlled subsidiaries in Canada and so it is not really Canadian capital. Nevertheless, according to a study by the U.S. Department of Commerce, foreign direct investment in the United States totalled $26.5 billion in 1974. Canada was the second largest investor, after Britain, with capital of $5.3 billion. The U.S. affiliates of Canadian corporations had total assets of almost $25 billion. Another study showed that Canadian corporations were leaders early in 1976 among foreign companies stepping up their investments in U.S. manufacturing industry.

According to the UN study, of the 650 largest corporations in the world, seventeen are based in Canada. This puts us sixth in the world-league table – but a poor sixth. The United States has 358 of the giants, Japan 74, Britain 61, West Germany 45, France 32 – and then Canada. The UN report listed 211 multinational corporations with sales exceeding $1 billion a year, but only two, Alcan Aluminium Limited and Massey-Ferguson Limited, were Canadian. It is also unfortunately true that Canadian multinational corporations tend to be in mining, banking, and the liquor trade rather than in manufacturing based on technological research and development. But this situation may be improving because the Canada Development Corporation, which was set up as an instrument of nationalism, has become, ironically, a multinational corporation with science-based interests. The CDC took over from the federal government ownership of Polysar Limited, a petrochemical producer with plants in Canada, the United States, West Germany, France, and Belgium and sales offices in seventeen countries. The CDC also controls Connaught Laboratories Limited, which is going into the business of manufacturing vaccines in Brazil, and has subsidiary interests in Denmark, Holland, and Mexico. The CDC's major coup, however, was in buying control of Texas Gulf Incorporated, a U.S.-based mining and natural resources development firm. In this way the CDC restored Canadian control over Texas Gulf's huge mining operations in this country. But it also became the controller of Texas Gulf's enterprises in the United States, Australia, and Mexico.

Multinational corporations are flourishing precisely because their size and flexibility gives them distinct advantages over national corporations. As the Gray report showed, they are financially strong because they can re-invest profits from subsidiaries and have access to money markets in several countries. They are able to take swift advantage of changing world conditions because they have production facilities in more than one country and sometimes in many countries. By switching production from one country to another, they can sometimes evade the control of national governments or at least put pressure on the government to give them a good deal. By exchanging goods and services within the corporation – for example, a subsidiary will buy from the parent company and sell to a subsidiary in another country – they bypass the competition of the free market and can more easily fix prices and profits. And, said the Gray study, the multinational corporation "is a long-run planning organization that realizes the value of central co-ordination and control. For instance, for the past several years, some one hundred major world corporations have been working on a study of the future corporate environment between the years 1975 and 1985 under the aegis of the Hudson Institute. Standard Oil of New Jersey has a group of executives looking at the global environment and its implications for the company in the 1980s and the 1990s. In contrast, the horizons of national governments tend to be limited by the length of their term of office."

In summary, multinational corporations are among the most dynamic and significant institutions of our times. They are already one of the main engines of economic growth in both developed and undeveloped countries, and they will become more important in the future. Their operations easily transcend national boundaries and the largest corporations have richer treasuries than many countries. They tend to develop and own the technology without which a modern economy cannot survive. Multinational corporations are here to stay and if Canada tried to expel them, or to nationalize their operations in Canada, it would be cutting itself off from the mainstream of international development. As the Watkins report said: "The multinational corporation is an economic and political reality of the modern world. Canada must come to terms with this fact of life."

Multinational corporations are not simply beyond the control of law. But they may have to be controlled by international law rather than by national governments. The United Nations, the Organization for Economic Co-operation and Development, the International Labor Organization, the European Economic Community, the International Confederation of Free Trade Unions, the World Confederation of Labor, the International Chamber of Commerce, and probably some other organizations are all currently studying the problem of how to control the multinational corporation. One of the most intriguing, although idealistic, suggestions is that instead of being chartered in a home-base country, the multinational corporations should be chartered by a UN agency. They would operate under international law administered by the United Nations and pay part of their taxes to the United Nations, making them truly multinational enterprises.

Balance of Payments

Foreign-owned corporations create payment problems for Canada by sending home the profits they make here and paying service fees to their parent corporations abroad. But that is only one side of the equation. They also export goods and services, very often to their parents and affiliates abroad, and these transactions bring money into Canada. The federal Department of Industry, Trade, and Commerce published in 1974 a report on the international operations of the larger subsidiaries in Canada in the period 1964-71. It showed that export earnings had been rising and roughly equalled foreign payments in the later years. There was a deficit of $205 million in 1969, a surplus of $145 million in 1970 and a deficit of $142 million in 1971 – small amounts in the total of Canada's balance of payments. But this is not to say Canada does not have a payments problem, or that foreign investment does not contribute to it. We have had a deficit in our current transactions with the rest of the world in twenty-one out of the past twenty-five years. The usual pattern has been to sell more goods abroad than we buy, but to spend more than we earn on services, such as payments of dividends and interest, royalties, copyrights, and tourism.

The bigger our debt to foreigners, the more money we have to send them. But when the world economy is strong, we can earn

187

enough from our exports of goods to meet the bills. When the U.S. economy was booming in the early seventies, we had surpluses in our balance of payments, for almost the first time since the Second World War, despite the fact that our foreign debt was already high. In the recession years of 1974 and 1975, we had large deficits. In short, foreign investment in Canada is only one factor in our balance of payments; and of course, many countries with much less foreign investment than Canada also run payments deficits – even the United States.

When we do have a deficit in our current payments it has to be covered in some way. Foreign capital coming into Canada is one way to meet the bill, but it is foolish to try to pay current accounts by selling capital assets, such as resources and industry, to foreigners. We have done that in the past but for the last three years the flow of direct investment has been the other way: more capital has been going out of Canada to buy industry and resources in other countries than has been coming in. We have more than covered our current accounts by borrowing abroad. When we borrow, we promise to repay, but sell nothing.

The essence of the matter is that by selling goods and services abroad and by investing in other countries we have to earn enough to pay for foreign goods and services and capital coming into Canada. To the extent that foreign capital makes us more productive and gives us access to world markets, it helps our balance of payments; to the extent that foreign subsidiaries don't export as much as they could, or buy supplies from sister companies abroad instead of purchasing in Canada, they hurt our balance. But we can make a similar statement about Canadian corporations: to the extent that they are efficient producers and aggressive exporters, they help; when they are inefficient, and poor salesmen, they are a hindrance.

The Gray report found little or no difference between the export performances of foreign and Canadian companies, but it did wonder why the foreigners, with their international connections, were not doing better. Turning to imports, the study found that foreign corporations tend to buy from abroad more than Canadian companies, and when they buy from parent or sister companies, they may not always get the best market price. But when the report tried to relate all this to the balance of payments,

188

it was frankly baffled: "In summary, it is evident that to determine fully the long-term impact of foreign direct investment on the Canadian balance of payments requires tracing through a series of direct and indirect consequences. Some efforts have been made to do this, but thus far this research does not permit precise qualification of the relationship." On balance, foreign investment probably does have an adverse impact on the balance of payments, but there are ways of dealing with the problem without banning investment.

Foreign Control

The more general fear about foreign investment is that boards of directors in other countries make decisions about their subsidiaries in Canada that are of vital importance to Canada but beyond our national control. This is true to a point. It is part of the price we pay for the efficiency of the supranational system that brings us many benefits. But the actual danger of foreign decision-making is often exaggerated.

Governments in Canada and abroad have their hands on what are called the big levers of economic management – the power to regulate taxes, the money supply, and, nowadays, incomes and prices. By stimulating or depressing the economy, governments create the economic climate in which businessmen make decisions about their operations. There is no evidence to suggest that foreign-owned and Canadian-controlled corporations respond in different ways to the influence of government policies. As both types of corporation are interested in the same goal, maximizing profit, it may reasonably be assumed that they respond in the same way. In short, it is governments and not corporations that make the vital decisions affecting the national and supranational economies.

THE NEW ECONOMIC SYSTEM

Having considered some of the problems associated with foreign investment, let us look at the reality of the world in which Canada has to find solutions. "One of the most significant recent trends in world affairs is the emergence of an integrated international economic system," said the Economic Council of Canada in its remarkable study of Canada's commercial prospects published in 1975. Significantly the report was called *Looking Outward*, and it is perhaps worth pointing out that the council is the most broadly based economic research institution in Canada. Although it was established by the federal government in 1963 and is financed by public funds, the membership of the council ensures that it is not merely a creature of the government. Among the members who signed the report were the president of the Canadian Labour Congress and five other union leaders, the heads of several major corporations, a couple of bankers, representatives of the agricultural industry, and a few distinguished citizens who, because they have no direct involvement in the operation of the economy, presumably represent the public. For the study of commercial policy, the council drew upon the work of fourteen members of the staff and nineteen outside specialists.

After more than three years of study and discussion, the council reached a consensus and published its report saying that the best policy for Canada in future would be to seek the widest possible degree of free trade, but if necessary to accept free trade with the United States alone. This proposal was extremely controversial, cutting across political positions and prejudices, and it is remarkable that a council representing such varied and conflicting interests could agree upon it. It is a fair assumption that the members of the council must have found the experts' description of the world, and of Canada's problems, so convincing as to overcome all differences.

It is this description with which we are concerned here because it is more realistic than the purely national perspective in which the problems created by foreign investment are normally considered. A solution to the problems has to take account of the world as it is and not merely as we might like to see it.

The Problem
The council detected "major trends of historic importance" in the international economic scene. The first of these is the shift in the economic balance. Some twenty years ago there were more than a score of advanced non-Communist countries, each with an essentially separate economy. There are today three superpowers – the United States, the European Economic Commu-

190

nity, and Japan. The second major change is the growth of regional trading blocs. Western Europe is already effectively a free-trade area, with contractual links to the Mediterranean area and to Africa. Two separate, common-market groups have been established in Latin America; the Commonwealth Caribbean countries have a free trade arrangement; and Australia and New Zealand enjoy modified free trade. In 1960, the size of Canada's domestic market was about average among industrial countries; by 1980 it will be less than one-quarter average size because most countries will be organized in free-trade areas. Canada will be one of the very few countries without free access to a market of more than a hundred million persons.

We shall also be facing new competition in manufacturing; a third great change going on in the world is the emergence of "new Japans," that is, countries just entering the industrial age and developing the sort of capacity for low-cost mass production of standard goods for which Japan was famous before the Second World War. In these countries, the choice for workers is between back-breaking labour in the fields and rice paddies for a subsistence living, or a production line in a modern factory for a wage that is perhaps very low by western standards, but much better than a handful of rice or corn. Hong Kong, Taiwan, India, Pakistan, Korea, Mexico, Brazil, Argentina, Iran, and Algeria are among countries now becoming industrialized, and others will follow. It is quite likely also that improvement of relations with the Communist world will bring to world markets a new flood of relatively low-cost manufactures.

The best response of the advanced western nations to these changes which increase the competitiveness of developing countries is in principle very clear, said the council: "They should shift resources away from labour intensive, standard technology production into areas in which they have greater comparative advantage by virtue of a more developed technology and highly educated work force." The shift means moving into what is called the post-industrial economy "in which the leading firms will not only be producers of goods, but generators of ideas as well," said the council. "Business enterprises in future will be increasingly research oriented and the most advanced countries will tend to develop and export technological know-how, follow-up services, and a variety of other intangible products in which the principal ingredient is intellectual capital." In other words, the post-industrial enterprise will deal not only in physical goods, but also in knowledge in one form or another. It will, for example, develop a new product in its research laboratories, provide the capital and the expert management to set up manufacturing plants in another country, and organize distribution and sales in international markets. The prime movers in this new and more efficient scale of production will be the multinational corporations because, as the council said, their "capacity for mobilizing resources and knowledge of global markets gives them the unique ability to produce almost anywhere and then distribute internationally." The council also said: "The most vital resource of all in the economy of the future probably will be managers, highly trained staff specialists, and other key personnel who can mobilize capital, people, and techniques (including technology, strictly defined) to the service of a profitable business venture. ... The newer management cadres will tend to head multinational firms."

This is the new world economy in which Canada must compete, and it's not going to be easy. We have some advantages: a well-educated population and natural resources. But we have plenty of disadvantages: a small domestic market which does not encourage mass production; high-cost labour and relatively poor productivity; a weak effort in research and development of new technology; and shortages of skilled managers and entrepreneurs. Some of these problems arise, as we have seen, from the high level of foreign ownership in Canada. But simply to encourage more Canadian control will not be the answer because it is clear that in the integrated international economy, the organization of production and distribution will transcend national borders. National economies will increasingly become cogs in a larger system. The country that wishes to prosper in the post-industrial world will have to accept the subsidiaries of foreign multinational corporations and create the conditions in which its own multinational corporations can operate in other countries. One of the costs in conventional terms will be the loss of some national independence.

The Gray report warned: "The growth of multinational enterprises is likely to lead to greater global integration of national economies. This will tend to reduce the abilities of national governments to control their own economic destiny." The Economic Council repeated: "The ability of all multinational enterprises to shift production facilities, technology, and research and management skills may tend to reduce the influence that individual governments can exercise over the development of their own economies." There is therefore a sort of *Catch-22* about the Canadian condition. The high level of foreign investment and control has weakened our ability to compete in the post-industrial world, but any attempt to ban further investment by multinational corporations, or to detach existing foreign subsidiaries from multinational connections, would make matters worse.

Answers
Both the Watkins and the Gray reports were extremely cautious in their recommendations and, in fact, really evaded the issue of what to do about foreign investment. Although the Watkins report has passed into folklore as a radical document, it was very far from that. Its main recommendation was for the establishment of a government agency to do further research into the activities of foreign subsidiaries and to co-ordinate federal policies toward them. It urged Canadians to recognize the importance of the multinational corporations and to encourage more of them to establish subsidiaries in Canada, and none of its recommendations would have had the purpose or the effect of reducing foreign investment. Its proposals were designed to see that Canada got the best return from foreign capital and technology.

The Gray study carried out much of the research recommended in the Watkins report and then reviewed various ways of tackling the problems raised by foreign investment. In conclusion it recommended that the federal government should establish an agency to review proposals by foreigners to invest in Canada to ensure that the investment would be of significant benefit to Canada. The government accepted this suggestion and the Foreign Investment Review Agency was established in 1974. It now reviews all proposals by foreigners to take over existing Canadian corporations or to start new corporations in Canada, and proposals by existing foreign-owned corporations in Canada to expand into new lines of business. The agency does not review expansion by existing foreign-owned corporations in their regular line of business, although this is the largest source of new foreign direct investment. The reason may be that if the agency were thought to be capable of assessing whether or not the expansion of existing foreign-owned corporations would be in the public interest, it would be equally capable, presumably, of assessing the expansion plans of Canadian-owned corporations. There would be a strong argument for bringing all private business investment plans under the scrutiny of the government to decide which would be in the public interest. While socialists would welcome such a scheme, others might think it too high a price to pay for national independence.

In reviewing foreign investment proposals the Foreign Investment Review Agency takes into account such considerations as whether the project will increase employment in Canada, bring new technology into the country, improve competition within the Canadian economy, involve Canadians in the enterprise as part-owners or managers, and whether or not it is compatible with national industrial and economic policies stated by the government. Where a proposal does not appear to the agency to be of significant benefit, the agency may bargain with the foreigner to persuade him to improve his terms, before recommending to the Cabinet whether or not to allow the investment. The Gray report made clear, and the government emphasized in establishing the agency, that the intention was not to reduce foreign investment, but to ensure that it entered Canada on the best terms. In its first two years of operation, the agency received 272 investment proposals and disallowed only 38 of them; in other words, it approved 80 per cent of the investment proposals made by foreigners as being of significant benefit to Canada. These statistics tend to confound those who welcomed the establishment of the agency in full confidence that when it began to investigate foreign investment it would find it not to be in Canada's interests. But the Gray report had warned that the review process alone would have little impact on the level of foreign investment and said: "The main burden for increasing the degree of Canadian ownership and control in the economy falls on various measures of a positive nature designed to support the development of Canadian entrepreneurship." The solution to the problem of foreign investment lies not so much in interfering with the inflow of foreign capital and expertise, but with measures to strengthen Canadian business and industry.

The Ontario Economic Council, which advises the provincial government, suggested a somewhat similar conclusion in a report on national independence published in 1976. The council was doubtful even about the activities of the Foreign Investment Review Agency, but said: "This report demonstrates that many but certainly not all the problems of national independence are caused by Canadian economic policies. It would likely be counterproductive to attempt to reduce foreign ownership without tackling the underlying causes inherent in existing Canadian policies."

The Economic Council of Canada in its report, *Looking Outward*, proposed the boldest solution. Instead of raising barriers against the outside world, it proposed to tear down existing barriers and to expose Canada to the widest possible degree of free trade. Best of all, said the council, would be world free-trade, but this was probably impractical. Second choice would be free trade with the United States, with Europe, and with Japan. Third choice would be free trade with the United States and Europe, or with the United States and Japan. But if necessary Canada should enter into a free-trade arrangement with the United States alone. Only in this way would Canadian industry be able to improve its efficiency and productivity by getting access to mass markets, on which an efficient manufacturing industry could be based, to lead Canada into the post-industrial world.

The council was keenly aware that the proposal would frighten many Canadian businessmen and outrage nationalists, and it tried to meet their arguments head-on:

Because much of Canada's secondary industry is at present relatively high-cost, the view prevails that a sharp decline in protection could lead to the demise of large parts of our manufacturing sector, leaving us with an economic system devoted mainly to primary production. Thus it is believed that our living standards would be reduced and that there would be insufficient employment for our work force. The result would be prolonged unemployment, large scale emigration, and a painful adjustment to the role of hewers of wood and drawers of water. Such fears are not well founded, in our view, since they are based on a conception of economic forces that is outdated and widely rejected by contemporary analysis. We are convinced that Canadian industry would be able to re-organize and prosper in a more freely trading environment – and in a manner that would provide very considerable long-run gains without a prolonged and painful adjustment process.

The council also examined what it called "the spectre of political union," the fear that a free-trade arrangement would lead to the political absorption of Canada by the United States: "This is the heart of the matter," it said. The council argued that the question would not be one of trading-in Canadian autonomy for dependence, because there was already a high degree of interdependence between Canada and the United States. The change would be largely from an unplanned North American economic relationship to a system based upon agreed rules of conduct in a free-trade treaty: "Indeed, it might be more realistic to argue that Canada's capacity for survival would be strengthened by accepting the fact that our unique trade relationship with the United States is irreversible. It would be better to deliberately define, in accordance with clear national objectives, the direction in which this relationship should develop, rather than to cope after the fact with the consequences."

The council did not endorse further foreign ownership in Canada; in fact it endorsed the efforts of the Foreign Investment Review Agency to keep direct investment inflows under review, and recommended exploring with the United States the possibility of adopting a set of guidelines on the behaviour of multinational enterprises. But it pointed out that it was Canadian tariff protection in the past that had encouraged foreign corporations to come into Canada to establish their operations, and it argued that a tariff-free market would give ample scope for accelerated development of Canadian innovative and managerial capacity and for the development of Canadian-controlled multinational corporations. "The long-run prospect, if free trade were adopted, is for a richer Canadian economy, less reliant on foreign capital and know-how to meet its investment needs," said the council.

This survey of the complex issue of foreign investment and national sovereignty reaches two principal conclusions:

We have no realistic choice but to accept a high degree of economic integration.

The solution to specific problems created by foreign investment lies not in attacking that investment or in raising barriers against the world, but in improving the ability of Canadian companies to compete in the emerging supranational system.

FOOTNOTES

Before leaving the subject let us try to clear up a few issues that often cloud debate on foreign investment.

The Level of Ownership

Many Canadians seem to imagine that foreign investors are continuing to gobble up an ever-increasing share of the Canadian economy, but this is not so. Foreign investment is growing but Canadian investment is growing faster, and the proportion of the Canadian economy owned or controlled by foreigners has actually been tending to decline in recent years.

The major source of information on the level of foreign ownership is the annual report on corporation finances made by Statistics Canada under the provision of the Corporations and Labour Unions Returns Act, known for short as CALURA. The Gray report used data from CALURA to establish that foreign-owned corporations owned 34.2 per cent of assets of non-financial industries in 1968. By 1971 the figure had risen to 37 per cent, but in 1972 it dropped to 35 per cent, and in 1973 it dropped slightly again to 34.3 per cent. In some sectors of industry foreign ownership and control is very much higher, and it is sometimes alleged that foreigners control all the vital industrial sectors. What is "vital" is a matter of opinion, but any list of industries of national importance would surely include financial institutions, transportation, communications, and public utilities. All these are owned and controlled almost exclusively by Canadians. Foreign ownership is most pronounced in the mining sector where it has dropped sharply from 69 per cent in 1971 to 58 per cent in 1973, principally because a few major firms changed from American to Canadian control.

Much of the concern about foreign investment concentrates on the manufacturing sector where the high technology industries are located, and here also there has been some decline in the level of foreign investment, from 59 per cent in 1971 to 56 per cent in 1973, although in some particular industries it is very much higher.

It does not follow that where there is heavy foreign investment there is necessarily "foreign domination." The oil and gas industry, for example, is largely foreign owned but it is closely regulated by provincial and federal governments. In other instances ownership may be divided between so many different foreign interests, American, European, and Japanese, that there is no effective control, let alone domination. If domination is taken to mean having more than 50 per cent control of an industry, the Gray report showed U.S. investors to be dominating only two major sectors of the economy, oil and gas, and mining and smelting.

The Gray report predicted that foreign investment in Canada would level off, and the most recent statistics suggest that is happening, although it is too early to establish a trend. It may well be that the problem of foreign investment is solving itself. The U.S. Ambassador in Canada, Thomas Enders, is not the most impartial source on economic relations, but he was probably right when he said in a 1976 speech:

> The great post-war inflow of U.S. direct investment to Canada is clearly over. In the early 1960s some $1 billion a year came in. Now for a number of years inflows (if you allow for price increase) are less than half as big. ... The recession year of 1975 was less than a quarter as big. ... The other side of these developments is growing Canadian direct investment in the States. Ten years ago such flows were insignificant, but in the 1970s they have greatly increased. Now Canadians are investing almost as much in the United States as Americans are in Canada.

This does not mean that foreign investment will not continue to grow in Canada; it means foreign subsidiaries are able to finance new investment out of profits and by borrowing within Canada instead of importing capital. According to the U.S. Department of

198

Commerce, u.s.-owned corporations invested almost $5 billion in Canada in 1975 and planned to increase the total in 1976. But Canadian corporations are also investing and expanding in Canada, apparently at a rate faster than the foreigners.

Zero Growth

This analysis has been based on the assumption we shall continue to seek industrial development and economic growth as major national goals. There is, of course, the contrary view that changing world circumstances will compel us to accept the so-called Stable State of zero growth. One theory is that Canada and other industrial countries will have to stabilize or even reduce their living standards in order to transfer resources to meet the rising demands of the less developed countries. Although such a new and fairer world economic order may be morally desirable and even inevitable in the long run, it is not likely to happen very rapidly. International relations and economic sharing are based as much on power as on moral principles, and the underdeveloped countries probably lack the cohesion to impose a united demand on the developed countries. It is hard also to see how a reduction in economic activity and consumption in the western world would necessarily help others who depend on the west for markets, capital, and technology, all of which are products of growth. There will no doubt be changes in the economic order over time, as there should be, but Canadians will strive to adjust to them without sacrificing their own standards and expectations.

Another scenario suggests that declining resources, increasing pollution, and the threat of an ecological disaster will force us into the Stable State. But the Club of Rome, which first gave credibility to the zero-growth-or-doomsday thesis, is now apparently modifying its view to say that moderate growth is not only possible, but desirable. It is instructive also to note that during the recent recession in which the developed democracies experienced a brief period of no-growth, the reaction was one almost of panic. National governments and international agencies, supported by almost all sectors of public opinion, strove to restore growth. So, although some political and opinion leaders are talking philosophically about less growth in the future, the priority in practice is maximum investment, development, and growth, and any realistic discussion of Canada's options has to recognize this reality.

If, however, we and other developed countries were to be forced by the demands of the Third World or by the approach of Doomsday to make drastic changes in our economic goals, it seems obvious that a very high degree of supranational planning and co-operation would be required, and this would probably infringe on Canada's sovereignty more rapidly than growth within the existing system.

A Post-Industrial Model

There is another possibility, seldom if ever discussed by nationalists, or by anyone else, for that matter. It is mentioned here only as a wistful personal postscript to the analysis of economic reality. The possibility is that we in Canada might voluntarily reject the goal of more industrial development and seek to build a different sort of economy on which to base a more satisfactory society. This is not to say we should reject growth; that would be quite unrealistic when there are many groups within Canada whose material needs remain to be met and when expectations remain high among even the relatively well-off. The scheme would be to turn the emphasis of development away from industry – factories, mills, refineries – and toward resources, particularly renewable resources, and such post-industrial activities as international financial services, scientific research, management expertise, tourism, and educational and artistic centres of excellence.

Our agricultural land, forests, and fisheries are immense resources certain to be in growing world demand. Water and water-power may become valuable and renewable resources. Exploration will probably produce new reserves of oil and gas and minerals beyond what we should need in an economy not seeking industrial growth. We have a highly educated population and the ability to attract qualified immigrants from other countries to work in the post-industrial service industries. Lack of development could become our greatest asset in an overdeveloped continent seeking rest and recreation. We could conceivably make our universities, medical centres, theatres, TV and film production studios, and publishing houses among the finest in the world, drawing students, scholars, artists, and customers from many countries.

Perhaps it is an idle dream. Perhaps a post-industrial economy can grow only out of an industrial economy that incubates the necessary capital and technology. But as far as is known, nobody has yet attempted to develop a model of the sort of economy described above to see to what extent it might be viable in Canada. Surely it would be worth the effort, for we know a good deal about the consequences of industrial development in our own country, and we can observe what has happened in the United States, Japan, and Europe. Along with the unquestioned benefits of affluence come problems of urban congestion, pollution, and human alienation.

We should not imagine, however, that a non-industrial Canada would enjoy any more sovereignty than a country developed in the conventional way. In fact, we should be locked firmly into the supranational system as a supplier of resources and services to industrial economies. But our quality of life might be better.

9

Culture and Identity

The Fathers of Confederation were sure that the Canadian society would be quite distinct from that of the United States, and of course superior. Canadians have been worrying almost ever since about whether they have succeeded in developing that separate identity, or whether they have been corrupted by American culture. We do not need to explore the entire record of national introspection. A couple of landmarks stand out.

Twenty-five years ago, the Royal Commission on National Development in the Arts, Letters, and Sciences (the famous Massey commission) reported its urgent concern about the impact of American influence in Canadian life, saying:

> Canadian achievement in every field depends mainly on the quality of the Canadian mind and spirit. This quality is determined by what Canadians think, and think about; by the books they read, the pictures they see, and the programmes they hear. These things, whether we call them arts and letters or use other words to describe them, we believe to lie at the roots of our life as a nation. They are also the foundations of national unity.

The Massey-report philosophy underpins a remarkable range of federal and provincial programs designed to protect and nourish Canadian theatres and films, galleries and museums, books and magazines, serious and popular music, and scholarship.

There is in addition legislation to restrain cultural competition from abroad. Foreigners may not own broadcasting stations, newspapers, or magazines. Television stations are restricted in the amount of foreign programming they can broadcast; that is, they must reserve time for Canadian programs. Radio stations must play a specified proportion of records judged to be "Canadian." Movie theatres are invited to show their public spirit by reserving a few weeks a year for Canadian films, and universities are pressured to hire fewer foreign professors.

A second landmark in the struggle to preserve identity was the formation and development of the Canadian Broadcasting Corporation. Intended originally to provide an alternative to U.S.-style radio broadcasting, it is instructed by Parliament to "safeguard, enrich and strengthen the cultural, political, social and economic fabric of Canada . . . and to contribute to the development of national unity and provide for a continuing expression of Canadian identity." The federal government alone spends well over $500 million a year to support culture and entertainment, and the provinces contribute substantial amounts. There is, of course, never enough money to support every cause. The CBC is starved of funds. Book publishers are always on the edge of bankruptcy. Magazines open and close. Major theatre companies are always economizing, and minor companies are always going broke. But despite these shortfalls, there has been an explosion of cultural activity in Canada in recent years, fueled in part by rising interest in nationalism. Canadian Basic Books, a catalogue produced with federal funds, listed more than 800 popular titles in 1976. The Canadian Periodical Publishers' Association reports there are more than 120 Canadian periodicals, although most are for small, specialized audiences. There are said to be 120 professional theatre companies and more than 3,000 professional artists at work across the country. The CBC and the private TV networks have been required by the Canadian Radio and Television Commission to show more domestically produced programs.

Yet, despite the fact that Canadian artists and entertainers in every medium have more opportunity than ever before to develop their talents, there is more concern than ever before about Canadian culture and identity. The explanation is that the culture and communication explosion in Canada has been only part of a greater explosion throughout the democratic world, and beyond. Canadian consumers are, therefore, more exposed than ever to foreign influences. Mass marketing of paperback books has made works of entertainment and enlightenment available in astonishing array. Affluence enables almost every citizen to possess a private concert hall – that is, a sophisticated sound system. Record and tape companies distribute every type of music. Jet travel encourages international distribution of periodicals and even daily newspapers. The average citizen may not go to the movie theatre as often as once he did, but TV enables him or her to see more films than ever, and pay-TV will soon permit selection of new movies for home showing. Above all, there is TV, the most compelling and pervasive form of communication ever invented.

According to A. W. Johnson, president of the CBC, in a 1976 speech, the average Canadian spends three hours and twenty minutes a day watching TV. Another report has suggested that some youngsters may spend as much as six or seven hours a day with an eye on TV– more time than they spend in school. Most of them can choose from a variety of channels, pulling the signals from the air or from cable that already reaches 50 per cent of the population and is expected to serve two-thirds by 1980. Many Canadian viewers can thus receive CBC in English or French or both; the privately owned CTV national network; the privately owned Global network in Ontario; one or two independent stations and perhaps a provincial educational station in major centres; some community programming from the cable company; the three private U.S. networks and the Public Broadcasting Service. The Canadian stations carry a good deal of U.S. programming; and according to Johnson, the average Canadian spends less than one-third of his viewing time watching Canadian programming. There is nothing much to be done about this: Canadians obviously enjoy foreign programming, and why shouldn't they? The U.S networks, with their huge domestic audience and worldwide export sales, are able to spend three times as much as the CBC, or even more, to produce an hour of programming. They are masters of professionally packaged entertainment, and their news services, although directed at U.S. interests, can often engage the attention of Canadian audiences. Senator Keith Davey, the chairman of the Senate Committee on Mass Media, which expressed profound concern about U.S. cultural penetration of Canada, has confessed that he regularly watches U.S. channels. Whenever there have been suggestions that the CRTC should forbid the spread of the cable system carrying U.S. networks to Canadian viewers, to reduce both the competitive pressure on Canadian broadcasters and the cultural impact on Canadian society, there have been loud public protests. "There is no point in pretending that we could roll back cablevision so as to force Canadians to watch Canadian programs," said Johnson. "Even if we wanted to, we couldn't. Canadians are accustomed to U.S. cable and they want it."

The CRTC has probably gone as far as it can, also, in imposing Canadian content on Canadian stations. "What is wanted," said Johnson, "is Canadian viewing of Canadian programs, not Canadian content that Canadians don't watch." In other words, forcing Canadian stations to show unpopular Canadian programs would merely persuade viewers to turn the dial to a U.S. station. So the CRTC has now taken a different and more realistic tack, by instructing cable companies to eliminate U.S. commercials from U.S. programs they receive. It is hoped to generate more advertising revenue in Canada to subsidize more and better TV production in Canada. In addition, the federal government has changed the tax law to encourage Canadian advertisers to buy time on Canadian stations instead of U.S. stations whose signals are received in Canada. The point is that there is no intention to reduce the amount of U.S. broadcasting *available* to Canadians. The most that is intended is that Canadian broadcasters will receive more revenue with which to make better programs to attract Canadian viewers.

But the goal for Canadian public and private broadcasters remains limited: "Our programming should become so good, and so worthy of being scheduled in prime time, that at least 50 per cent of the viewing time of Canadians will come to be spent watching Canadian programs rather than American ones," said Johnson. He added: "A goal simply stated, but so difficult to achieve!" Difficult indeed, and perhaps impossible because an improvement in Canadian programming is likely to be matched by the increasing variety and quality of foreign programs available to Canadians. Ironically, it is the U.S. Public Broadcasting System that is already bringing to Canadians some of the best of British programming – drama, documentary, and comedy.

As costs rise, there seems also to be a trend toward multinational co-operation in program production. The CBC is reported to be in partnership with TVO in Ontario (the provincial educational station), BBC in Britain, and PBS in the United States to make a series of programs on economics starring John Kenneth Galbraith, the former Canadian who became an American and is now the best-known economist in the world. According to some futurists, satellites will soon make it possible to receive TV programs from all over the world, and Canadians would then have a choice not of a dozen channels carrying programs from two or three countries, but of scores of channels carrying programs from every continent. There is no reason at all why Canadian TV producers should not play a vigorous and growing role in the emerging supranational system of communications. We ought to be able to make programs of the highest quality that will appeal not only to Canadian audiences, but also to U.S. and other foreign audiences. American companies earned $130 million from foreign sales of TV programs in 1973. British sales have risen sharply to about $60 million a year; in 1975, the BBC alone exported about 9,000 hours of programs, and private producers in Britain sold more.

If Canadian productions do not have similar international appeal, huge subsidies will be required to produce for the small Canadian market alone. But even if we can raise the quality and the quantity of Canadian production, both private and public, it is not likely to be so good and so relevant to all Canadians as to drive out the best of programming from the rest of the world. In short, Canadians are certain to continue watching a vast amount of foreign TV, mostly American, but probably with an increasing contribution from other countries.

Much the same will be true of other branches of popular culture. (High culture is universal almost by definition; classical music, art, and literature know no borders.) Canadians will have available to them more books written in Canada, more Canadian magazines, more Canadian movies, more Canadian music and theatre. But these Canadian expressions will not be a dominating influence on Canadian life and attitudes because of the quality and quantity of art and entertainment available from foreign sources. As the Ontario Economic Council noted in its pamphlet, *National Independence:*

> Canadians seem to be as concerned – perhaps even more concerned – with cultural independence as they are with foreign ownership. Notwithstanding the sincerity of the concern or the range of the difficulties, the fundamental reality of the situation must be defined and acknowledged. Canada is a nation of 22.7 million people, of whom roughly six million have French as their mother tongue. This leaves less than 17 million English-speaking Canadians, most of whom reside at intervals along a strip several thousand miles long and extending, more or less, one hundred miles north of the American border. In most areas of Canada the population density is low. On the south side of the border there are over 210 million Americans. . . . If Canadians watch television programs broadcast in the United States and intended for American audiences, or listen to u.s. radio stations, the money cost to Canadian consumers is zero and the u.s. listeners incur no cost. Given that most people in Ontario live in close proximity to u.s. radio and television stations, they are bound to receive a variety of u.s. programs at zero cost. In contrast, with an English language population of 17 million, Canada cannot provide equivalent programming except at a very high cost. Most Canadian media industries face similar problems.

This statement expresses the central economic fact about the development of Canadian culture. And unless we are prepared to close the border by jamming the airwaves and banning the import of books and magazines, the situation will continue. Such drastic action is unthinkable for at least two reasons. It would run counter to our liberal and democratic tradition of free access to ideas and information, and it would be rejected by the great majority of Canadians who thoroughly enjoy access to foreign entertainment.

In summary, the existing organization of culture and communications makes available to Canadians an extraordinary variety of art and entertainment, without stifling Canadian artists who are continuing to develop. The remaining concern is the absence of a distinctive Canadian culture that reflects and nourishes a distinctive Canadian society with values different from those of the United States.

A DISTINCT SOCIETY?

The Fathers of Confederation had a conservative vision of Canada. Unlike the founding fathers of the United States, they were not concerned with writing idealistic manifestos or inventing new models of democratic government. "They thought of themselves as British subjects, and assumed they were the legitimate heirs of the British constitutional heritage and full participants in the British political experience," wrote Donald Creighton in *Canada's First Century*. He added: "Constitutional monarchy, parliamentary institutions and responsible government made up a political tradition which was not only British but also British American. The Fathers of Confederation assumed, without question, that this political tradition must be continued unimpaired in the nation they were creating." They had, said George Grant, the philosopher, in his book, *Lament for a Nation*, "an inchoate desire to build, in these cold and forbidding regions, a society with a greater sense of order and restraint than freedom-loving republicanism would allow. It was no better defined than a kind of suspicion that we in Canada could be less lawless and have a greater sense of propriety than the United States."

The United States was a liberal society, believing that if individuals were allowed equal opportunity to fulfil themselves with the minimum interference from government, the better side of human nature would triumph and out of the competition of private interests would come the maximum public good. The Canadian society was conservative, concerned to preserve the established community with the Crown at its head, respectful of tradition and slow to change, looking to religion for moral prescription to curb the dark side of man's nature, and seeking, above all, order and stability. The difference, said W.L. Morton, the historian, in his book, *The Canadian Identity*, is that the U.S. constitution promises life, liberty, and the pursuit of happiness, whereas the British North American Act speaks of peace, order, and good government. Gad Horowitz, in his well-known essay defining that distinctive Canadian political animal, the "Red Tory," says succinctly: "What is un-American about British Canada can be summed up in one word: British." But the vision of a Canadian society based on British conservative principles has faded as Britain itself has faded. Few would now seek to model Canadian society on British society, or even to attach much importance to the British connection, and when they do, the effort is self-defeating. The Crown has become a symbol more of disunity than unity; it is resented in Quebec and has little appeal to younger English Canadians, an increasing number of whom come from countries other than Britain. The Commonwealth stirs no passions or loyalties.

In fact, said Grant, the attempt to build a conservative society in Canada has failed. His book, *Lament for a Nation,* is subtitled *The Defeat of Canadian Nationalism.* In it, he wrote, "The impossibility of conservatism in our era is the impossibility of Canada. As Canadians we attempted a ridiculous task in trying to build a conservative nation in the age of progress, on a continent we share with the most dynamic nation on earth. The current of modern history was against us." British conservatism, he said sadly, provided Canada with political and legal institutions, but not with a distinctive way to organize an industrial society: "Conservatism must languish as technology increases. It was not conceivable that industrial society would be organized along essentially different principles from those to the south." He was prepared even to concede that the absorption of Canada into the United States might be for the best. One of the arguments for continentalism, he noted, is that, "In moving to larger units of government, we are moving in the direction of world order. If Canadians refuse this, they are standing back from the vital job of building a peaceful world. After the horrors that nationalistic wars have inflicted on this century, how can one have any sympathy for nationalism?" How indeed?

To explore Grant's thinking in search of his answer is dangerous; he has warned in another context against "impertinent precis written by those who think they can say in fewer words what wiser men than they have said in more." But his book of essays, *Technology and Empire* – a more difficult and profound work than *Lament,* which is half political polemic – suggests that what he was lamenting is not the passing of a Canadian nation, but of that conservatism that linked man to the roots of his civilization in Athens and Jerusalem. He could not articulate what "good" has been lost to man in the technological society: "All languages of good except the language of the drive to freedom have disintegrated, so it is just to pass some antique wind to speak of goods that belong to man as man," he said in a descriptively despairing phrase. But he suspected darkly that some vital quality has been lost, that change is not progress, that the disappearance of Canada will be just a small milestone on man's march to the ultimate tyranny of the universal, homogeneous, technocratic state. It is a chilling view, but not of much help in this discussion. We cannot repeal the Age of Progress and the industrial revolution.

In lamenting the loss of conservatism, however, it is just possible that Grant wept too soon. Throughout the industrial democracies there appears to be a substantial reaction against technology and development, and a desire to return to a simpler way of life in local communities governed by values associated with earlier times. To what extent this attitude will actually change society is impossible to say, but it is interesting to note that the movement had its origins in Europe and the United States in the work of such writers as Jacques Ellul *(The Technological Society),* Lewis Mumford *(Myth of the Machine),* and the missionary of the counterculture, Charles Reich *(Greening of America).* The idea of a "conserver society" came later to Canada, as many fashions do, and certainly can't be claimed as a national distinction that sets us apart from others.

If we cannot oppose Canadian conservatism to American liberalism, how about socialism? Many nationalists do call themselves socialists, ranging from revolutionaries in far-left splinter groups to democratic reformers on the right wing of the New Democratic Party. But there is not in Canada a significant socialist movement that seriously promises to transform the society by abolishing capitalism. The Regina manifesto, which proposed to eradicate capitalism, introduce socialized planning, and turn Canada into a co-operative commonwealth, died with the CCF party. The CCF's successor, the NDP, merely promises, from election to election, to reform in a modest way the existing institutions. The leaders may declare, and their followers may believe, that the ultimate goal is still socialism, undefined, but the reality is that in order to have a chance of being elected, the party's platform must always be so mild as not to alarm the great majority of Canadians who are reasonably happy with their society. The NDP, far from proposing a distinctive society, offers a version of the welfare state based on a mixed economy not much different from that of the Liberals and Progressive Conservatives.

In a provocative chapter of *Political Parties in Canada,* Conrad Winn and John McMenemy argue that regardless of what parties may say about the welfare state and the redistribution of income, they act in office in similar ways. The NDP provincial governments are no more radical than governments formed by other parties. Certainly the NDP dare not propose to do what would be essential to the creation of a socialist state in Canada in present circumstances: to close the border with the United States to prevent the flight of capital and people; to nationalize at least the major foreign-owned corporations in order to sever their multinational connections and to bring them under direct control; and to impose the will of the central socialist government on reluctant provinces.

So in preaching national independence the object is not to build a different society now, but to preserve the status quo – that is, to resist economic and cultural integration – in the hope that one day, some day, Canadians will see the light and welcome the socialist dawn. The point was frankly made by Gad Horowitz in an article in the left-wing magazine *Canadian Dimension,* some ten years ago on why Canadian socialists should be nationalists. To diminish the economic and cultural influence of the United States, he wrote, it was necessary not to preserve some unique set of Canadian values but "to preserve the possibility of building, in this country, a society which is better than the Great Society. It needn't be uniquely Canadian as long as it isn't a copy of the United States. It could be anything." He repeated that the overriding purpose was to retain "Canada's freedom of action to become something – who knows what it will be – different from Flint, Michigan."

We are still waiting for that vision of the better Canada to clarify, and meantime the NDP concentrates on fighting its chosen devils, the multinational corporations, which it sees, correctly, as one of the major instruments of economic and social integration. But integration into what? Most of the industrial democracies in Western Europe already have social democratic governments. In the United States there is much criticism of corporate power, and even *Time* magazine asked on the cover of its edition of July 14, 1975, "Can Capitalism Survive?" The magazine thought it could, but others are not so sure. Among American authorities who have written recently on the subject, Daniel Bell has described the *Cultural Contradictions of Capitalism,* Robert Heilbroner has analysed *Business Civilization in Decline,* Michael Harrington has perceived *The Twilight of Capitalism,* and the most influential economist of the age, Galbraith, has explored the *New Industrial State* and prescribed socialist remedies.

In short, the supranational system of industrial democracies is probably entering a post-capitalist era. No one can foretell the future, but one can theorize that the liberalism, which is the ideology of private enterprise, is dying because it has become clear that the consequences of setting the freedom of the individual above the needs of the community are uncontrolled economic growth, leading to pollution and depletion of resources, and the erosion of the shared values that bind a society. There is a widely felt need to turn back to some form of collectivism that takes account of community needs and values. Conservatism is probably unacceptable because tradition and religion have lost their mystic authority to prescribe standards. The democratic alternative is collectivism that arises from public debate, decision and consent – which would be socialism at least to the extent of ensuring greater public control over private economic behaviour. Canadian socialists, or social democrats, meanwhile, spend their energies in fighting to preserve Canada's illusory independence and freedom to be "different" in some unspecified way.

It remains true, however, that Canada is now more progressive than the United States. Our welfare state is more highly developed, and we have had a long experience with state ownership of industries that are expected to serve public good rather than private profit. In his book *A Nation Unaware, the Canadian Economic Culture,* Herschel Hardin, the Vancouver playwright, critic, and broadcaster, argued that public ownership distinguishes the Canadian political culture from the U.S. culture. He sought to show that ever since the building of the Lachine Canal in 1821, Canadians have relied on public enterprise and finance to play a leading role in economic development. Not only have many of these Crown corporations – CNR, CBC, Ontario Hydro, Air Canada, Polymer, and others – enjoyed periods of great success in the past, said Hardin, but they are models for the world's future. In the Stable State that he foresees, public monopolies will make more sense than private enterprise because they will avoid wasteful competition and be content with public service rather than growth. Canadians fail to recognize the value of their public enterprise culture, said Hardin, only because, like good colonials, they have been conditioned to admire the U.S. model of private enterprise.

It is easy to pick small holes in Hardin's large canvas: public enterprise was often a second choice forced upon reluctant Canadians because private enterprise was not available; Crown corporations tend to degenerate into examples of state capitalism, having the same goals as private corporations, but without the discipline of profit and competition; nationalized corporations are not as inefficient as critics make out, but not always as innovative as Hardin implies (given a choice, customers sometimes prefer private to public enterprise service); it is one thing to establish a Crown corporation and another to keep it under effective public control; and so on. Hardin also tended to underestimate the amount of public enterprise in the United States. The Quebec government built the Lachine Canal, as he says proudly, but the U.S. government built the Panama Canal, and the U.S. Corps of Engineers has constructed dams and other public works on a significant scale. We have the CBC, and the U.S. now has PBS.

Nevertheless, there is truth in Hardin's picture, but it explains more about the past than the future. Public ownership is only one means by which governments exercise control over the economy, and not the most important means even in Canada. There is a trend toward government planning and direction of the economy in all industrial democracies, including the United States, and in that respect our political cultures are becoming more alike rather than more distinct.

The truth may be that the technologies of travel, communication, manufacture, and distribution impose a way of life on Canadians that is not much different from the way of life in other advanced industrial countries. For example, working in a factory in Canada is very similar to working in a factory in the United States. The lifestyle is reflected in the popular and political cultures which, accordingly, are increasingly alike. It follows that if we wish to create in Canada a culture distinct from that of the United States, we shall first have to build a distinctly different economy. But as the previous chapter showed, far from becoming more distinctive, our economy is becoming more integrated into those of the other democracies.

This is perhaps the place to acknowledge that this argument has concerned itself only with English-Canadian culture. Protected to some extent by their language, French Canadians have been more successful as film-makers, TV producers, and popular entertainers. But if the Quebec culture is "national" in the sense that it is homemade and reflects French-Canadian experience and environment, it does not appear to an outsider to reflect a new and different society. We seem to see a North American society markedly different from English Canadian and U.S. society only in that it speaks French.

CANADA AND THE U.S.

If we cannot identify distinctly Canadian virtues we can always criticize U.S. vices and reject the model of U.S. society. It is not difficult, but criticism is often exaggerated and hypocritical. The war in Vietnam was offered as proof that the United States was a cruel, imperial power out to enslave the world, including Canada. In fact, it was just another in the long, bloody history of conflicts between nations, unusual because it was ended not by victory or defeat, but by free Americans who rejected canting appeals to patriotism and national destiny, and used the democratic process to force their leaders to make peace. The Watergate scandal, in its turn, was accepted as evidence of corruption in the American society and proof of the inferiority of the

American political system. A less complacent way to view events would be to say that American democracy proved more vigorous and successful in exposing and punishing political wrongdoing than has sometimes been the case in Canada. Similarly, when Canadians describe the United States as a racist society, they choose to forget the problems of the Canadian Indians, the history of English-French bigotry in Canada, and the treatment of Chinese, Indian, and Japanese immigrants in this century.

It is worth remembering also that when Canadians are not exposing American decadence, they are very often espousing ideas and causes that grow out of the vigorous American society. Such fashionable concerns as the liberation of women, militant consumerism, and the slowing of growth to protect the environment have all spread into Canada from the United States. The protest against the war in Vietnam started not with Canadians rejecting U.S. values, but with Americans who sought change in their own society. Indeed, it is hard to think what would engage the energies of Canadian activists if there were no American causes to copy!

The mass distribution and powerful influence in Canada of U.S. films, television, books, and magazines is sometimes attacked as cultural imperialism. The problem, however, is not imperialism, but technology which has broken down barriers and jumped borders. If Canadians are going to accuse Americans of imposing their culture upon us, they had better consider what they and their technology have done to others. French-Canadian culture is disappearing outside Quebec and the adjacent areas of Ontario and New Brunswick. The way of life of native people in southern Canada has been almost destroyed, and the same process is probably inevitable in the north. It is fashionable to talk romantically about preserving native lifestyles, but it is nonsense to suppose that 20 million southern Canadians will refrain from exploiting the oil and gas and minerals in the north in order to leave the territory to Indians and Eskimos living in a traditional way on a huge reserve fenced off from the industrial world. The issue is not whether the north will be exploited, but when and on what terms. With exploitation will come southern culture, and the most natives can hope for is time to adapt to it. It may already be too late. Tagak Curley, executive director of the Inuit Cultural

215

Institute, complained to the CRTC in 1976 that the CBC Northern TV Service was providing fourteen communities with sixteen hours of programming a day: thirty minutes a week was in the language of the Inuit. Curley appealed to the CRTC to "preserve the Inuit culture from the devastating impact of southern media." So much for cultural imperialism. The history of civilization is in large part the story of cultures superseding each other. Sad, no doubt, but true, and unlikely to change.

The United States is an imperial power in the sense that it sees itself as responsible for the security of the Free World, so called, which usually means those countries that share American ideas or protect American interests. As one might expect of an imperial power, it occasionally acts in nakedly imperialistic ways. Canada and other countries in the Free World view the situation with ambiguous feelings. We are glad to be under the security umbrella, but we resent imperialism when it imposes on us, and disassociate ourselves when it is directed against others. There is no sensible alternative, however, to our association with the United States. We are not neutral in the conflict between the United States and the Communist empire. We are not a poor and underdeveloped country, with coloured citizens and an African or Asian culture, able to identify with the Third World; we are a rich country exchanging goods and services on a huge scale with the United States to which we are also tied by history, language, and millions of private associations between individuals.

When we denounce U.S. imperialism we ought also to keep in mind that, half a century ago, we were enthusiastic supporters of the leading imperial power, Britain, and that less than forty years ago, we criticized U.S. isolationism and reluctance to become involved in foreign wars. Times change, and will again. Meanwhile, the growth of the supranational system embracing Western Europe and Japan creates counterweights to the United States, which are perhaps our best chance to avoid absorption.

THE REAL CHOICE

We are locked into a supranational economy and a supranational culture that serve our interests reasonably well; independence could be attained, if at all, only by making drastic changes in our way of life, which would be unacceptable to

216

almost all Canadians. But this is not to say we have no identity. Identity depends on a sense of belonging, on a piece of land or in a society, and not on political independence. Quebeckers have maintained their identity in Confederation; Scots have maintained their identity in the United Kingdom; Canadians are maintaining identity in the supranational system, which is already well developed.

We must intensify our efforts to ensure that our artists have the fullest opportunity to develop their talents, our scholars the resources to learn and to teach – expecting not that they will invent a new national culture, but that drawing on their different environments and experiences in Canada, they will make their own distinctive contributions to the supranational culture. Nor does economic integration mean we no longer have national interests to protect. Of course we do. Even as national states decline, they remain competitors in some degree for wealth and influence. We must continue to manage Canada's internal affairs and external relations with skill and determination if we are to earn a fair share of the world's wealth and to exert influence in the world's councils. We have, for example, to arrange our public finances and private businesses so as to be competitive in trade. We have to bargain shrewdly over tariffs and other trade barriers to ensure we get the best economic advantage, and we have to make sure that we get the best return from foreign capital invested in Canada and from Canadian capital invested abroad. We have to strike a realistic balance between conserving resources for our own use and sharing them with others, because our prosperity is dependent on the prosperity of trading partners.

Within limits, we can also set our own social priorities, redistributing income, reorganizing social services and education, reforming political institutions, and so on. But the limits are that we shall not be able to go much faster – or much slower – than the other countries within the system. Economic competition imposes its own discipline, and mass communication establishes what is socially and politically acceptable throughout the system. These are requirements for survival in a world that is changing, but in which the national state will remain an important institution for some years to come.

But what really matters is how we adjust to the supranational society that is emerging – not throughout McLuhan's Global Village, but in that wealthy section of the village in which we are fortunate to live. Nationalists say the choice is between vigorously asserting Canadian sovereignty and becoming a wholly-owned colony of the United States. But as the discussion has shown, this is to put the issue in out-of-date and therefore misleading terms, because there can be no truly independent countries when the organization of economic activity, the popular culture, and social values transcend national borders.

The real choice for Canadians is what role to play in the new supranational society. Shall we struggle to preserve whatever remains of national sovereignty, raising barriers against foreign influence, searching anxiously for a national identity and finding it mainly in dislike or even hatred of our neighbours? Or shall we welcome the opportunity offered by the new supranational society, take the lead in lowering national barriers even further, and invite other countries to join with us in the adventure of building a democratic political system that transcends national borders and matches the reality of our economic and cultural lives?

If we allow ourselves to be exhausted and frustrated by efforts to achieve the impossible goal of national independence, we may find ourselves in a few years forced to apply late in the day, on unfavourable terms, for membership in a supranational system we have had no hand in designing. Or worse, a serious international crisis arising from threat of war or economic depression may drive us helter-skelter without forethought into the embrace of the United States. The alternative is to take a leading role in promoting and designing the supranational system to ensure that we are not merely junior partners in North America, but major actors in a society that embraces all the industrial democracies.

It would be naive to believe that the institutions to govern such a society will be built easily or quickly, and it would be presumptuous to suggest in any detail what form they should take or what Canadian policy should propose. There are already a number of multinational institutions in place. The North Atlantic Treaty Organization provides the forum in which governments co-ordinate their defence policies and, to a lesser extent, their foreign policies. The Organization for Economic Co-operation and Development provides for the co-ordination of economic policies. Canada also has an extraordinary range of bilateral links with the United States, documented by the Senate Committee on Foreign Affairs in its 1975 report, *Canada-United States Relations, The Institutional Framework for the Relationship.* There have been sixty-one meetings between prime ministers and presidents in the past half-century. One-to-one communication between Canadian and U.S. ministers, personally or by phone, "have been increasing and are now an accepted way of doing business." The Canada-U.S. Joint Ministerial Committee on Trade and Economic Affairs has met thirteen times since 1953. The number of contacts between officials "is enormous," and the senators suggested that in addition an informal committee of top civil servants from both countries should meet occasionally to discuss current issues. Provincial governments maintain relations with neighbouring states, and the senators were surprised to discover there were "766 agreements, understandings or arrangements in effect between Canadian provinces and American states by 1974." The International Joint Commission adjudicates boundary disputes and now has the important task of monitoring joint efforts to reduce pollution of border waters; the Canada-United States Inter-Parliamentary Group brings together legislators from both countries. Much of this is in addition to routine diplomatic relations carried on through embassy channels. These elaborate official arrangements have evolved over the years to regulate the personal and commercial relations that bind the two countries with millions of ties across what is almost an open border for many purposes. There are about 70 million border-crossings a year. One-third of all the goods produced in Canada are sold in the United States; the United States sells to Canada more than it exports to all the countries of the European Economic Community. About a million people born in Canada now live in the United States; about 400,000 Americans have moved to Canada. Canada's ties to Europe are on a different scale, but significant and becoming stronger. We share with Britain a monarch, a system of government, an association in the Commonwealth, even our constitution. Millions of Canadians have family connections in Britain, and there are of course growing numbers of Canadians – Italians, Germans, Portuguese, and many others – with personal and cultural ties to countries on the continent of Europe. The new Quebec strives to identify with France and its former colonies. The Trudeau government has signed a "contractural" agreement with the European Common Market precisely in order to balance ties to the United States. The rising importance of Japan is recognized by the new emphasis in foreign policy on the so-called Pacific Rim, and there is an arrangement for occasional joint meetings of Japanese and Canadian ministers in a sort of binational cabinet committee.

The existence of the multinational and binational arrangements is an acknowledgement of the high degree of interdependency that already exists. The weakness is that the arrangements have grown up in a haphazard way; they lack a central body to provide direction and co-ordination. The danger is that contacts are usually between executives – ministers and bureaucrats – and are not subject automatically to review and consent by elected representatives. It could be argued that concealed in the web of official contacts, we have in effect a supranational executive, but no supranational parliament to which it is accountable. Each national government, of course, is responsible to its national legislature, but the big picture of shared interests and commitments escapes attention.

What is now required is the vision and the political will to begin forging all these *ad hoc* arrangements for consultation into a central body with power to make decisions, for which it would be responsible to a central legislature. The federal principle would obviously prevail, as it did at Confederation and in the U.S. constitution; that is, national states would surrender sovereignty over those matters that are of common importance while retaining control of matters of only local concern. A supranational government – probably made up of delegates from national governments and supervised by a parliament elected by national legislatures – might eventually be responsible for foreign relations and defence; broad economic strategy; regulation of trade and commerce, including the operation of multinational corporations, to ensure free movement of people, capital, goods, and services within the system. Local states might retain control over regional economies, education, social services, the administration of law, and the protection of civil rights – in short, those things that are rooted in local tradition and contribute some distinction to the quality of local society.

A dream? Of course, but so was Confederation, and so have been most great adventures in nation-building. But there is also a certain logic about the concept of the supranational state. Man first organized his affairs through the family. Families joined in tribes. Tribes became races occupying nation states. Next came the national states embracing several nations. Now we must move on to the supranational state, which brings together several national states that have come to share an economy and a culture. Those who refuse to think beyond the limits of our present borders, who believe it disloyal even to contemplate a state greater than Canada, lack both perspective and imagination. They ignore the past and fear the future. Our heritage was not invented by the Fathers of Confederation. For those of us of European descent, it goes back to Greece and the Holy Land; for the native peoples, it goes back to Asia. Our destiny surely cannot depend on the maintenance of a political organization created over a century ago in circumstances utterly different from those today. It is nobler to hope that our destiny may lie in leading others to build a federation that fits today's circumstances – a great enterprise to equal the vision of the Fathers of Confederation who struggled to tear down colonial barriers to build a new society in their time.

Bibliography

Adam, G. Stuart. *Journalism, Communication and the Law.* Toronto: Prentice-Hall of Canada Limited, 1976.

Adams, Ian; Cameron, William; Hill, Brian, and Penz, Peter. *The Real Poverty Report.* Edmonton: M.G. Hurtig Limited, 1971.

An Energy Policy for Canada. Issued under the authority of the Minister of Energy, Mines and Resources. Ottawa: Information Canada, 1973.

An Energy Strategy for Canada. Issued under the authority of the Minister of Energy, Mines and Resources, 1976.

A Science Policy for Canada. Reports of the Special Senate Committee on Science Policy, 1970, 1972.

Bagehot, Walter. *The English Constitution.* Introduction by R. H. S. Crossman, MP. London: The Fontana Library, 1963.

Bell, Daniel. *The Cultural Contradictions of Capitalism.* New York: Basic Books, Inc., 1976.

Broadbent, Ed. *The Liberal Rip-Off.* Toronto: New Press, 1970.

Clement, Wallace. *The Canadian Corporate Elite.* Toronto: McClelland and Stewart Limited, 1975.

Constitution of Canada. Final Report of the Special Joint Committee of the Senate and of the House of Commons, 1972.

Creighton, Donald. *Canada's First Century.* Toronto: Macmillan of Canada, 1970.

Crozier, Michel J., Huntington, Samuel P., Watanuki, Joji. *The Crisis of Democracy.* New York: New York University Press, 1975.

Diefenbaker, John G. *One Canada. The Crusading Years 1895 to 1956. The Memoirs of the Right Honourable John G. Diefenbaker.* Toronto: Macmillan of Canada, 1976.

Economic Council of Canada. *Fifth Annual Review.* Ottawa: Queen's Printer, 1968.

Economic Council of Canada. *Looking Outward.* Ottawa: Information Canada, 1975.

Economic Council of Canada. *People and Jobs.* A study of the Canadian Labour Market. Ottawa: Information Canada, 1976.

Ehrbar, A.F. "Looking Back on a Decade of Misery," *Fortune* Magazine, February, 1976.

Ellul, Jacques. *The Technological Society.* Translated from French by John Wilkinson. A Vintage Book distributed in Canada by Random House of Canada Limited, 1964.

Foreign Direct Investment in Canada. Report of the (Gray) working group, 1972.

Foreign Ownership and the Structure of Canadian Industry. Report of the (Watkins) Task Force, 1968.

Galbraith, John Kenneth. *Economics and the Public Purpose.* Boston: Houghton Mifflin Company.

Guide to the Guaranteed Income. Prepared by the office of the National Council of Welfare, Ottawa, 1976.

Grant, George. *Lament for a Nation.* Toronto: McClelland and Stewart Limited, 1965.

Grant, George. *Technology and Empire.* Toronto: House of Anansi, 1969.

Green, C., Cousineau, J.M. *Unemployment in Canada: The Impact of Unemployment Insurance.* The Economic Council of Canada, 1976.

Hacker, Andrew. "What Rules America," *The New York Review of Books,* May 1975.

Hardin, Herschel. *A Nation Unaware.* Vancouver: J.J. Douglas Limited, 1974.

Harrington, Michael. *Socialism.* New York: Saturday Review Press, 1972.

Heilbroner, Robert H. *Business Civilization in Decline.* Toronto: George J. McLeod, 1976.

Horowitz, Gad. *Red Tory.* In Canada, *A Guide to the Peaceable Kingdom.* Toronto: Macmillan of Canada, 1970.

Income Support and Supplementation. By officials of the Federal-Provincial Working Party on Income Maintenance, 1975.

Jackson, Robert J. and Atkinson, Michael M. *The Canadian Legislative System.* Toronto: Macmillan of Canada, 1974.

Jones, Aubrey. *The New Inflation.* London: Andre Deutsch, 1973; New York, Penguin Books, 1973.

Knowledge, Power and Public Policy. A study for the Science Council of Canada by Peter Aucoin and Richard French, 1974.

224

Johnson, Paul. "A Brotherhood of National Misery," *The New Statesman*, May 16, 1975.

Lewis, Robert. Interview with John Kenneth Galbraith. *Maclean's Magazine*, February 9, 1976.

Lippmann, Walter. *Public Opinion.* Toronto: Collier-Macmillan Canada Limited, 1922.

MacKay, R.A. *The Unreformed Senate of Canada.* Toronto: McClelland and Stewart Limited, by permission of the Oxford University Press, 1963.

March, Roman R. *The Myth of Parliament.* Toronto: Prentice-Hall of Canada Limited, 1974.

Maxwell, Grant. *Attitudes at the Canadian Grassroots.* Ottawa: Distributed by Social Affairs Office, Canadian Catholic Conference, 1975.

Morton, W.L. *The Canadian Identity.* Toronto: University of Toronto Press, second edition, 1972.

Ontario Economic Council. *National Independence.* 1976.

Perspective Canada. Prepared in the office of the Senior Adviser on Integration, Statistics Canada. Published under authority of the Minister of Industry, Trade and Commerce, 1974.

Poor kids. A report by the National Council of Welfare, Ottawa, 1975.

Porter, John. *The Vertical Mosaic.* Toronto: University of Toronto Press, 1965.

Poverty in Canada. A report of the Special Senate Committee. Ottawa: Information Canada, 1971.

Prices and Incomes Commission. Final report on inflation, unemployment and incomes policy. Ottawa: Information Canada, 1972.

Rogaly, Joe. *Parliament for the People.* London: Maurice Temple Smith Limited, 1976.

Siebert, Fred S.; Peterson, Theodore; and Schramm, Wilbur. *Four Theories of the Press.* Illinois: University of Illinois Press, 1956.

Smith, Denis. *Gentle Patriot.* Edmonton: Hurtig Publishers, 1973.

Stewart, Walter. *Divide and Con.* Toronto, New Press, 1973.

The Institutional Framework for the Relationship. The Standing Senate Committee on Foreign Affairs, Canada-United States

Relations, Volume 1. Ottawa: Information Canada, 1975.

"The New Concerns About the Press," *Fortune Magazine,* April, 1975.

The Uncertain Mirror. Report of the Special Senate Committee on Mass Media. Ottawa: Queen's Printer, 1970.

Towards a Mineral Policy for Canada. Opportunities for Choice. Published under authority of the Federal and Provincial Ministers responsible for mineral policy. Ottawa: Information Canada, 1974.

Winn, C., McMenemy, J. *Political Parties in Canada.* Toronto: McGraw-Hill Ryerson, 1976.

Work in America. Report of a Special Task Force to the Secretary of Health, Education, and Welfare. Cambridge, Massachusetts: MIT Press, Cambridge, 1973.

Working Paper on Social Security in Canada. Published by Marc Lalonde, Minister of National Health and Welfare, 1973.

Index

and state control, 75
Medicare, 47, 95
MPS, 22, 28, 30, 32, 51; and elections, 25
Mercantilism, 84
Métis, the, 162
Mexico, 185, 191
Middle East, the, 181; and oil, 175
Military, the, and young people, 148
Mills, C. Wright, 140
Milton, John, 74
Mineral reserves, 171-72
Minerals, 200, 215
Minimum income, 13
Ministry of State for Science and Technology, 179
Minorities, 16
Mixed economy, 106
Monarchy, 57
Montreal, 172
Morris, Joe, 114, 115, 116, 118
Morton, W. L., 208
Motivation and profit, 156
Motivation and Personality (Maslow), 144
Moynihan, Daniel P., 66
Multinational Corporations in World Development (UN study), 182-83, 185
Multinational enterprises (MNES), 184; and advantages, 182-87; and production, 191-93
Multinationals, 182-87
Mumford, Lewis, 210
Muzak, 156
Myth of the Machine (Mumford), 210
Myth of Parliament, The (March), 22, 28-29

Nation Unaware, the Canadian Economic Culture, A (Hardin), 213
National Board for Prices and Incomes, the (Britain), 100

National Council of Welfare, The, 126, 129, 136, 146, 147
National Energy Board, 173, 174
National Independence (Ontario Economic Council pamphlet), 207
National Revenue Dept., 135
Nationalism, 165; and its weaknesses, 167
Nationalists in Canada, 167
Natural Gas, 172, 174, 175, 198, 215
Natural resources, 141, 175
Negative income tax, 136-37
Nestle, 183
New Brunswick, 56, 57, 215
NDP, 116, 210-11, 212
New Economy, 139
New Glasgow, 131
New Industrial State (Galbraith), 212
New Inflation – The Politics of Prices and Incomes, The (Jones, 100, 120
New Society, definition of, 9
New Statesman, The, 115, 117, 182
New York Review of Books, The (Hacker), 122
New York Times, The, 69
New Zealand and its electoral system, 27
Newfoundland, 161
Newspapers and labour, 78
Newsweek, 66
Nixon, Richard, 36, 65, 66, 67, 110, 173
Norman Wells, 172
North Atlantic Treaty Organization (NATO), 163, 218
Northern Electric, 178
Norway and worker-directors, 158
Nova Scotia, 56

Obsolescence, 95
Official Languages Act, 48

Provinces, the, and their jurisdiction, 62
Provincial government, and revision, 59
Provincial governments, their growth, 42
Provincial powers, 42
Public Broadcasting Service, 204
Public Broadcasting System, 206
Public control vs. private control, 160
Public Opinion (Lippmann), 70
Public ownership, 155
Public service corps, 148-49
Public spending, extravagant, 134
Puritan society, 14

Quebec, 37, 41, 42, 43, 45, 48, 49, 50, 51, 52, 56, 57, 172, 209, 214, 215; and elections, 25; and MPS, 27; and press councils, 75
Queen's University, 88, 120
Question Period, 25, 33, 35, 59
Quiet Revolution, 42

Racism, 215
Rasminsky, Louis, 107
Rationing, 15
Raynauld, André, 102, 105, 116, 118, 133
Real Poverty Report, The, 125
Recession, 19
Regina Manifesto, 210
Reich, Charles, 210
Reid, John, 24
Reisman, Simon, 98, 99, 100, 110
Reporters and government, 70
Research and development, 169
Resources, 15; renewable, 200
Revenue, National Dept. of, 60
Revolution, The, 11
Rideau Hall, 38
"Rights of poverty," 152
Rogaly, Joe, 22, 26
Rowcliffe, Katherine, 18
Royal Commission on Bilingualism and Biculturalism, 43

Royal Commission of Corporate Concentration, 158
Royal Commission on National Development in the Arts, Letters, and Sciences (Massey Commission), 202
Royal Commission on the Press (Britain), 75
Royal Commission on Taxation (Carter Commission), 132

St. Laurent, Louis, 71
Sarnia, 172
Saskatchewan,51, 52, 172
School of Journalism (Carleton), 72, 75
Schreyer, Ed, 116
Science Council of Canada, 179
Scientific knowledge, 15
Seaway workers, 101
Securities regulations, 45
Senate, 36-39, 40, 59-61, 62
Senate Committee, 74, 75, 76, 81, 125, 126
Senate Committee on Foreign Affairs, 219
Senate Committee on Mass Media, 73, 205
Senate Committee on Poverty, 125, 127, 129
Senate Committee on Science Policy, 119, 176, 177, 178
Senate-Commons Committee, 43-45, 47, 48, 56
Senators, 37, 61
Separatism, 48
Seventies, the, 150, 165
Shaw, Bernard, 78
Sixties, 9, 16-17, 20, 87-88, 99, 101, 103, 107, 165, 175; and full employment, 149
Smith, Adam, 84, 85
Social democrat, 11, 212
Social justice, 124
Social services, 44
Social welfare, 131
Social welfare programs, 136

ment, 36; inflation, 92; integration with Canada, 163; and investment in Canada, 168-69; and investments, 135; and oil in Canada, 172-73; and the press, 66-69; and press councils, 75; and research and development, 177; and its trade policies, 180, 181; and worker investment, 158
University of Chicago, 135
University of Toronto, 98
Unreformed Senate of Canada, The (Mackay), 37
Upper House, 37, 38
Urban planning, 42

Venezuela, 172
Vertical Mosaic, The, (Porter)), 10, 72, 76, 77, 140
Vietnam, 67, 71, 214, 215

Wage and price control, 83, 92
Wall, D. F., 31
War of Independence (American), 161
Washington Post, 69
Watanuki, Joji, 17
Watergate, 67, 69, 71, 214
Watkins, Mel, 168
Watkins report, 168, 169, 170, 176, 177, 180, 181, 184, 193
Welfare, 42, 87, 136
Welfare state, the, 13, 136, 137, 212
West, the, 51, 55
West Germany, 188; and worker-directors, 158
Whig capitalism, 14
Wilson, Phyllis, 79
Winn, Conrad, 64, 211
Women and the labour force, 140-41
Woodcock, George, 166, 167
Work, and change; 144-45; definitions of, 145-46, 149; and the environment, 144, 153-55; and goals, 144; and motivation, 144;

as "paid employment," 145; and satisfaction, 144; and social responsibility, 143; in the U.S., 143; and workers, 152-53
Work attitudes, 141
Work ethic, the, 142-145
Work in America, 153
Worker, the, 139-60
Workers and work, 152-53
Working Paper on Social Security in Canada (federal government), 146
Workmen's Compensation, 130
World Conference of Labour, 187
World War I, 85
World War II, 86, 149, 164, 172, 191

York University, 89, 100, 119
Young people, 140; and employment, 140; and the labour force, 139-40; 141; and unemployment, 150; and work, 142, 143